DK EYEWITNESS TRAVEL

TOP 10
ATHENS

CORAL DAVENPORT
AND JANE FOSTER

Penguin
Random
House

Top 10 Athens Highlights

The Top 10 of Everything

CONTENTS

Athens
Area by Area

Streetsmart

**The information in this DK Eyewitness
Top 10 Travel Guide is checked regularly.**
Every effort has been made to ensure that
this book is as up-to-date as possible at the
time of going to press. Some details,
however, such as telephone numbers,
opening hours, prices, gallery hanging
arrangements and travel information are
liable to change. The publishers cannot
accept responsibility for any consequences
arising from the use of this book, nor for any
material on third-party websites, and cannot
guarantee that any website address in this
book will be a suitable source of travel
information. We value the views and
suggestions of our readers very highly.
Please write to: Publisher, DK Eyewitness
Travel Guides, Dorling Kindersley, 80 Strand,
London WC2R 0RL, Great Britain, or email
travelguides@dk.com

Within each Top 10 list in this book, no hierarchy
of quality or popularity is implied. All 10 are,
in the editor's opinion, of roughly equal merit.

Front cover and spine The Erechtheion, Athens
Back cover The Acropolis, Athens
Title page Temple of Apollo, Delphi

Welcome to
Athens

Ancient temples. World-class museums. Mediterranean sunshine and deep-blue skies. Sandy beaches and waterside nightclubs. Athens brings together the best of ancient and contemporary Greece. It is dynamic, hedonistic and exhilarating, and with Eyewitness Top 10 Athens, it's yours to explore.

We each have our own image of the magnificent **Parthenon** upon the **Acropolis**: an ancient temple in a modern European capital. But it's not until you arrive in Athens that you realize how seamlessly the Ancient Greek monuments and ruins are integrated into Athens' contemporary urban life. Marble columns and beautifully carved pediments lie scattered in an Arcadian meadow next to a busy metro station – this is the **Agora**, at Monastiraki. The **National Archaeological Museum**, a proud Neo-Classical building, is filled with hoards of invaluable centuries-old treasures next to a street where walls are spray-painted with political slogans, on the edge of Exarcheia. But Athens relishes these parallel worlds, and nothing is forbidden.

The city sprawls in a wide valley, protected by rugged mountains, and opening to the south on to the glistening Aegean Sea. From the dense conglomeration of concrete apartment blocks rise two peaks: the aforementioned Acropolis and **Lykavittos Hill**, a rocky mound capped by a tiny church, which is enchantingly floodlit at night. And it is after dark that the city celebrates its passions for eating, drinking and flirting with life.

Whether you are coming for a weekend or a week, our Top 10 guide brings together the best of what this ancient city has to offer. There are insider tips throughout, from the best things to do for free to sights off the beaten track, along with extensive lists of hotels and restaurants, and nine easy-to-follow itineraries. Add inspirational photography and detailed maps, and you have the essential pocket guide. **Enjoy the book, and enjoy Athens.**

Clockwise from top: **Odeon of Herodes Atticus; Osios Loukas mosaic, Delphi; Brettos, Plaka;** view of the Acropolis; Piraeus Cathedral; Olympic Stadium; National Archaeological Museum

Exploring Athens

Athens offers a vast range of things to do and see, both ancient and modern. Here are some ideas of how to make the most of your time. The city centre is relatively compact, so you should be able to do most of your sightseeing on foot, without resorting to public transport.

Colourful Plaka is the place to shop for traditional souvenirs.

Two Days in Athens

Day ❶

MORNING

Begin with Athens' centrepiece, the **Acropolis** (see pp12–13), crowned by the Parthenon. See finds from the site at the ultra-modern **Acropolis Museum** (see pp14–15), then lunch at the museum café.

AFTERNOON

Follow the **Dionysiou Areopagitou walkway** (see p60) around the Acropolis to the **Agora** (see pp16–19). Walk to **Plateia Monastiraki** (see p86), calling at **Melissinos Art** (see p89) for made-to-measure sandals, then hunt for souvenirs in **Plaka** (see p79).

EVENING

Dine on contemporary Greek fare in the hip **Gazi** (see p90) neighbourhood.

Day ❷

MORNING

Look in the colourful **Central Market** (see p94; closed Sun), then visit the **Museum of Greek Gastronomy** (see p88; closed Mon). Walk up Ermou, stopping at **Kapnikarea** church (see p87), to Syntagma, home to the **Parliament** (see p101). Walk through the **National Gardens** (see p101) to the **Benaki Museum** (see pp26–7; closed Mon–Tue). Lunch in Kolonaki.

AFTERNOON

Walk, or take the cable car, up **Lykavittos Hill** (see p102) for fabulous

Key
━━ Two-day itinerary
━━ Four-day itinerary

The Parthenon sits above the Acropolis hill, overlooking Athens.

Day ❷
MORNING
See the **Kerameikos** *(see pp30–31)* archaeological site, then wander through the colourful **Central Market** *(see p94; closed Sun)*. Walk up Ermou, stopping at the church of **Kapnikarea** *(see p87)*, then proceed to Kolonaki.
AFTERNOON
Visit the **Byzantine and Christian Museum** *(see pp32–3)*. Browse the shops in Kolonaki, refuel with coffee, then check out the nearby **Museum of Cycladic Art** *(see pp22–3; closed Tue)*.

Day ❸
MORNING
Visit the **National Archaeological Museum** *(see pp20–21)*.
AFTERNOON
Catch the tram to **Glyfada** *(see p129)* and relax on the beach. If it's too cold to swim, head for the thermal waters of **Lake Vouliagmeni** *(see p129)*.

Day ❹
MORNING
Visit the **Museum of Greek Musical Instruments** *(see p78; closed Mon)* in Plaka. Explore **Filopappos Hill** *(see pp34–5)* and the **Temple of Olympian Zeus** *(see pp36–7)*, then walk through the **National Gardens** *(see p101)* to Kolonaki.
AFTERNOON
Visit the **Benaki Museum** *(see pp26–7; closed Mon–Tue)*. Hike up **Lykavittos Hill** *(see p102)* for views over the city.

city views, then cross Exarcheia to arrive at the **National Archaeological Museum** *(see pp20–21)*.
EVENING
After an aperitif at the **TAF** bar-gallery *(see p82)*, have dinner in Plaka, below the floodlit Acropolis.

Four Days in Athens

Day ❶
MORNING
Begin with the **Acropolis** *(see pp12–13)*, followed by the ultra-modern **Acropolis Museum** *(see pp14–15)*.
AFTERNOON
Proceed to the **Agora** *(see pp16–19)* for more ancient history, then explore the cafés and souvenir shops in pretty **Plaka** *(see p79)*, also checking out the **Roman Forum and Tower of the Winds** *(see pp24–5)*.

Top 10 Athens Highlights

The Parthenon, on the Acropolis

TOP 10 Athens Highlights

Athens is both the Classical, marble-pillared cradle of Western civilization and a modern urban sprawl of concrete and traffic. Between these extremes lies a vibrant city, where the influences of East and West entwine in the markets, cafés and tavernas, which are built upon ancient ruins and rub shoulders with gold-leafed Byzantine churches.

Acropolis ①

The crown jewel of Greece, if not all of Europe. Its temples are the most influential buildings in Western architecture (see pp12–15).

② The Agora

The likes of Socrates, Aristotle and St Paul all held forth in the marketplace below the Acropolis. This was the heart of the ancient city (see pp16–19).

③ National Archaeological Museum

Finds from some of the world's greatest cultures are housed here. Exhibits include the gold treasure of Mycenae and the first sculptures to depict the complexity of the human form (see pp20–21).

④ Museum of Cycladic Art

This museum houses the largest collection of Cycladic art in the world, showcasing the culture of a matriarchal island whose 5,000-year-old icons still inspire artists of the modern world (see pp22–3).

⑤ Roman Forum and Tower of the Winds

The Romans abandoned the ancient Agora and created this orderly new commercial centre. Its showpiece was the magnificent Tower of the Winds (see pp24–5).

ÍPEIROU
LIOSION
ACHARNON
MARNI
3 SEPTEMVRIOU
VATHIS
PLATEIA VATHIS
MARNI
KAROLOU
AGIOU KONSTANTINOU
PLATEIA OMONIA
OMONIA
PLATEIA KOTZIA
AIOLOU
(PEIRAIOS)
SOFOKLEOUS
GAZI
TSALDARI
PLATEIA ELEFTHERIAS
EVRIPIDOU
IERA ODOS
PANAGI
AG. ASOMATON
DIPYLOU
PLATEIA IROON
ATHINAS
AIOLOU
ERMOU
PSIRI
ERMOU
PLATEIA AVISSYNIAS
PLATEIA MONASTIRAKI
APOSTOLOU
② MONASTIRAKI ⑤
ASYRMATOS
PAVLOU
Areopagus Rock
ANAFIOTIKA
Hill of the Nymphs
DIONYSIOU
AREOPAGITOU ①
⑨
MAKRIGIANNI
VEIKOU

Benaki Museum 6
This first-rate collection of Greek art from Neolithic times to the present is housed in a beautifully renovated Neo-Classical mansion, with an intriguing history and a famed rooftop view (see pp26–7).

Kerameikos 7
Classical Athens' cemetery gives a fascinating cross-section of life, and death, at the city's edge, with elaborate tombs, temples, sacred roads – and an ancient brothel (see pp30–31).

Byzantine and Christian Museum 8
The rich history of the Byzantine Empire is told through the greatest examples of its works, from the intricacy of precious metalwork to the solemnity of the many icons (see pp32–3).

Filopappos Hill 9
A green-gladed respite in the city centre, with a wonderful view and a mix of monuments ranging from ancient and Byzantine to modern (see pp34–5).

Temple of Olympian Zeus 10
Ancient Greece's most colossal temple stands beside the monumental arch that divided Athens between Greek hero Theseus and formidable Roman emperor Hadrian (see pp36–7).

🏆 Acropolis

The temples on the "Sacred Rock" of Athens are considered the most important monuments in the Western world, for they have exerted more influence on our architecture than anything since. The great marble masterpieces were constructed during the late 5th-century BC reign of Perikles, the Golden Age of Athens. Most were temples built to honour Athena, the city's patron goddess. Still breathtaking for their proportion and scale, both human and majestic, the temples were adorned with magnificent, dramatic sculptures of the gods.

① Acropolis Rock
As the highest part of the city, the rock **(main image)** is an ideal place for refuge, religion and royalty. The Acropolis Rock has been used continuously for these purposes since Neolithic times.

⑥ Erechtheion
Poseidon and Athena are said to have battled for patronage of Athens on this spot. The Erechtheion's design combines temples to each of the two gods **(above)**.

② Temple of Athena Nike ("Victory")
There has been a temple **(above)** to a goddess of victory at this location since prehistoric times, as it protects and stands over the most vulnerable part of the rock.

③ Propylaia
At the top of the rock, you are greeted by the Propylaia, the grand entrance through which all visitors passed to reach the summit temples.

④ Panathenaic Way
The route used in an ancient procession during which a new tunic, or *peplos,* would have been offered to Athena, along with sacrifices.

⑤ Parthenon
The epitome of ancient Greek Classical art, a magnificent "Temple to the Virgin", goddess Athena **(left)**. She was represented inside by a giant gold and ivory sculpture.

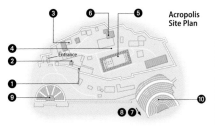

Acropolis Site Plan

7 Panagia Chrysospiliotissa

Originally dedicated to the god of wine and revelry, the cave was later turned into the church of the Virgin of the Golden Cave.

8 Acropolis Museum

The stunning Acropolis Museum *(see pp14–15)* houses around 4,000 artifacts within a space almost 10 times larger than the old museum.

9 Odeon of Herodes Atticus

A late addition to the Acropolis, built in 161 by its namesake. In summer it hosts the Athens Festival *(see pp72–3)*.

THE ACROPOLIS IN LATER TIMES

In the 5th century AD, the Parthenon was used as a church. During the Ottoman occupation, it was used as a mosque, and the Erechtheion as a harem. The Ottomans also kept gunpowder in the Parthenon, which led to its near destruction when the Venetians shelled it in 1687 *(see p35)*. The Parthenon suffered further damage in 1799 when Lord Elgin removed sculptures, architectural features and inscriptions, taking them back to England.

10 Dionysus Theatre

This mosaic-tiled theatre **(below)** was the site of Classical Greece's drama competitions, where the tragedies and comedies by the great playwrights were performed. It seated 15,000, and you can still see engraved front-row marble seats, reserved for priests of Dionysus.

NEED TO KNOW

Acropolis: **MAP J5** ■ 210 321 4172 ■ www.culture.gr

Open 8am–8pm daily

Adm €20; students half price. A special €30 ticket allows entry to Kerameikos, Theatre of Dionysus, Agora, Roman Forum, Temple of Olympian Zeus, the Lyceum and Hadrian's Library (valid for 5 days)

Acropolis Museum: **MAP K5** ■ Dionysiou Areopagitou 15 ■ 210 900 0900 ■ www.theacropolis museum.gr

Open Apr–Oct: 8am–8pm Tue–Thu, Sat & Sun (to 4pm Mon & 10pm Fri); Nov–Mar: 9am–5pm Mon–Thu (to 10pm Fri & 8pm Sat & Sun).

Adm €5

■ Visit first thing in the morning or at sunset to avoid the midday heat and multitudinous tour groups that arrive in droves late morning.

Acropolis Museum

The Caryatids

 The Caryatids
The original statued pillars that supported the Erechtheion's porch have been brought inside. Their arms are broken now, but initially they held libation bowls.

2 The Parthenon Marbles
The marbles are displayed in the order in which they would have graced the Parthenon, with blank spaces significantly left for sculptures that remain in London.

3 The Calf-Bearer
This joyous Archaic sculpture shows a bearded man carrying a calf, to be offered as a sacrifice to Athena. The statue itself was a votive offering and dates to 570 BC.

 The Peplos Kore
One of the most exquisite of the Archaic votive statues. Her gown, called a *peplos*, was painted with decorative colours. Traces of paint are still visible on her eyes, lips and curly hair.

5 Kore with Almond-Shaped Eyes
The most sumptuous of the votive *koroi* – her detailed drapery and fully formed body show real development in sculpture. Her dress was painted with detailed patterns, including a border with the distinctive "Greek key" pattern.

6 Pediment of the Ancient Temple
Part of the pediment of an ancient temple to Athena, built before the Parthenon and later destroyed, shows Athena fighting against a Giant. It dates to 520 BC.

7 The Kritios Boy
This sculpture of a young male athlete marks the transition from Archaic to early Classical sculpture, with the introduction of a naturalistic pose. The Kritos Boy sculpture dates to 480 BC.

The "Mourning Athena"

8 Relief of the "Mourning Athena"
This tiny relief shows the goddess Athena as a girl, without sword or shield and clad in an Attic *peplos*.

9 The Glass Floor
The museum has been built directly over an early Christian settlement. Glass floors allow visitors to look directly down into the site while surrounded by Classical and Archaic sculptures.

10 Frieze on the Temple of Athena Nike
The small but dynamically sculpted frieze shows scenes of battle, with gods, Persians and Greeks all stepping into the fray.

MORE THAN A BUILDING

Parthenon marble

The small, worn-around-the-edges museum that used to be linked to the Acropolis had never really done justice to the stunning treasures it held within. But the newer, all-glass showpiece of a museum at the foot of the Acropolis does. The old museum closed in July 2007 in anticipation of the move to the Acropolis Museum, which opened mid-2009. However, there was an ulterior motive to the construction of this museum, which was to send a pointed international message. In 1799, the seventh Earl of Elgin removed two-thirds of the sculptures of gods, men and monsters adorning the Parthenon and took them to England. Most were sold to the British Museum, which refuses to return them, saying that the sculptures are integral to its role in narrating human cultural achievement. The Acropolis Museum has answered previous criticism that Athens could not display them adequately or safely, for a special room awaits the return. Greece hopes that when thousands of international visitors see the sparkling but empty showcase, it will increase the pressure on Britain, forcing a much-anticipated return of the marbles.

TOP 10
SCENES DEPICTED IN THE PARTHENON MARBLES

1 The birth of Athena, springing fully formed out of Zeus's head (see p46)

2 The Pantheon watching Athena's birth

3 Athena and Poseidon's fight for control of the city (see p46)

4 The gods watch and take sides in Athena and Poseidon's battle

5 The Panathenaic Procession, ancient Athens' most important religious event

6 The battle of the Centaurs and Lapiths

7 The battle of the gods and the Giants

8 The battle of the Greeks and the Amazons

9 The sack of Troy

10 Priestesses prepare a veil for Athena

At the Acropolis Museum, glass walls allow a direct view of the Acropolis temples from within the museum, while the glass floor offers a view over the ruins of an early Christian settlement.

🔟 ⭐ The Agora

Athens' ancient marketplace, founded in the 6th century BC, was the heart of the city for 1,200 years. It was the centre for all civic activities, including politics, commerce, philosophy, religion, arts and athletics. This is where Socrates addressed his public, where democracy was born and where St Paul preached. Because of its varied uses, the rambling site can be confusing. Compared to the sweltering Acropolis, the grassy Agora is a relaxing place to wander, as you imagine the lively bustle that once filled this historic centre.

1 Temple of Hephaestus

The best-preserved Classical temple in Greece (above), devoted jointly to Hephaestus and Athena. Its fantastical frieze depicts the deeds of Theseus and Herakles.

Agora Site Plan

2 Tholos

The executive committee of the first parliament lived and worked in this circular building. The name translates as "beehive".

3 Odeon of Agrippa

Marcus Vipsanius Agrippa, an official with the first emperor Augustus, had this theatre built in AD 15. Outside stood statues of three serpent-tailed Giants and Tritons on huge plinths (left). Two Tritons and a Giant remain.

4 Stoa Basileios

Built in 500 BC, this building housed the office of legal affairs concerning ancient cults. Most of it was destroyed when the Goths invaded Athens in AD 267. Its ruins are best viewed from Adrianou.

⑤ Monument of the Eponymous Heroes

Citizens were divided into 10 tribes (phylae), each represented by a different Attican hero. Dated 350 BC, this monument had bronze statues of each representative tribal hero: Antiochos, Ajax, Cecrops, Hippothoon, Erechtheus, Aegeus, Leos, Akamas, Pandion and Oeneus.

⑥ Middle Stoa

The large Middle Stoa **(above)** took up the major part of the central marketplace, its aisles lined with Doric columns.

⑦ Altar of Zeus Agoraios

This lavish temple to the ruler of the gods was originally built elsewhere in Athens (possibly the Pnyx) in the 4th century BC. In the first century AD, it was dismantled, brought to the Agora and reconstructed.

⑧ Nymphaion

The ruins of the Nymphaion, an elaborate 2nd-century fountain-house, are still visible, despite the building of a Byzantine church over it in the 11th century.

⑩ Great Drain

When Athens experiences a downpour, the Great Drain **(above)** still collects runoff from the Acropolis and Agora, and sends it to the now mostly dry Eridanos river.

SITE OF PILGRIMAGE
You may well see people standing on the Areopagos, the rock above the Agora, praying or singing hymns. Pilgrims from around the world retracing the steps of Paul converge here, the site named in the Bible (Acts 17:22–34) where the saint gave his famous "Men of Athens …" speech. The address spoke of the wrongs of ancient Greek religions, and here Paul converted the first Athenians to Christianity.

NEED TO KNOW

MAP B4 ■ Adrianou, Monastiraki ■ 210 321 0185 ■ www.culture.gr

Open 8am–3pm daily Times are subject to change, so call ahead to confirm

Adm €8, or included in €30 Acropolis ticket

■ The best overview of the Agora is from the Areopagus rock (see p61).

■ Head to the local favourite Dioskouroi, situated on the street of the same name. It serves coffee and snacks, with outdoor tables lined along scenic steps.

⑨ Stoa of Attalos

King Attalos II of Pergamon (159–138 BC) built this impressive two-storey structure **(above)**. It was reconstructed in 1956 by the American School of Archaeology. Today the Stoa is a world-class museum displaying finds from the Agora (see pp18–19).

Agora Museum (Stoa of Attalos)

1 Aryballos
This small Archaic oil-flask sculpted in the form of a kneeling boy represents an athlete binding a ribbon, a symbol of victory, around his head. It dates to around 530 BC.

2 Klepsydra
Dating back to the 5th century BC, this is a unique example of the terracotta water clocks used for timing speeches in the public law courts. When a speaker began, the stopper was pulled out of the jug. It would take exactly six minutes for the water to run out, at which point the speaker had to stop, even if he was in mid-sentence.

Klepsydra

3 Ostraka
These small inscribed pottery fragments played a crucial role in the incipient democracy. Called *ostraka*, they were used as ballots in the process of ostracism. When there was fear of a tyranny, citizens voted to exile politicians considered dangerous to democracy. Those displayed show the names of several prominent politicians exiled in this way, including Themistokles, one of Athens' most important leaders.

Ostraka fragments

4 Bronze Shield
This huge Spartan shield was a trophy taken by the Athenians after their victory over the Spartans in the battle of Sphacteria, in 425 BC. It is a vast object, and it is difficult to imagine a soldier carrying something so heavy and cumbersome into the melee of battle. On the front of the shield, one of the Athenian victors has inscribed, "Athens defeated Sparta at Pylos".

5 Head of Nike
This small, delicate head of Athena Nike, dated to about 425 BC, was once covered with sheets of silver and gold; eyes would have been inset.

6 Winged Nike
This sensuous, swirling, rippling statue of Athena once adorned the Agora's Stoa of Zeus Eleutherios. Her active stance and clinging, flowing *chiton* (a loose, full-length tunic) are typical of the way in which the goddess was depicted at that time. It dates to around 415 BC.

7 Apollo Patroos
This colossal but finely sculpted marble cult statue of Apollo graced a temple to the god in the Agora. A later copy shows that in this sculpture the god of music was playing the kithara, an early stringed instrument. Dating to around 330 BC, it is the work of the famous Greek sculptor and painter Euphranor.

Apollo Patroos

8 Athenian Law for Democracy
In 336 or 337 BC, the citizens of Athena passed a historic vote for a new system of democracy, giving

every (male) citizen an equal vote. The law is inscribed here, and topped by an image of a personification of the Demos (people) of Athens being crowned by Democracy herself.

 Marble Kleroterion
This device was used by the Parliament of Athens between the 3rd and 2nd century BC, in the period of the ten tribes of Attica, to select people randomly for official roles. The seemingly simple box performed operations with slots, weights, cranks and coloured balls. A sign below the display case explains the complexities of its operation.

10 Calyx Krater
Dating to 530 BC, this is the earliest known calyx krater – an elegant vessel used to mix water and wine at banquets – and the only vase of this shape attributed to Exekias, the greatest Attic vase painter. It shows several beautifully detailed scenes, including Herakles being introduced to the gods of Olympus and the Greek and Trojan heroes' fight over the body of Patroclus.

THE STOA OF ATTALOS

The Stoa of Attalos was originally a 2nd-century BC shopping mall. Both arcades were divided into shops, and the cool marble-pillared space was a popular place for wealthy Athenians to meet and gossip. Through decades of excavations, the Agora has become recognized as one of Greece's most important sites, yielding finds precious for their artistic quality and ability to tell important stories about political and cultural life in the first democracy. In the 1950s, the American School of Archaeology reconstructed the Stoa and converted the building into a museum to display finds from the site. Most of the museum's exhibits are closely connected with the development of democracy in Athens. Outside, in the marble passage, statues that once adorned the temples in the marketplace are displayed.

Head of Nike

The reconstructed Stoa of Attalos, home of the Agora Museum

⑩⭐ National Archaeological Museum

More than just the best museum in Greece, this is one of the most important and exciting museums in the world. It is packed with famous, influential and beautiful works, from the Neolithic Age, to the great Bronze Age cultures described by Homer, to the Golden Age of Classical Athens, up to the Roman era. Highlights include the numerous gold artifacts found at Mycenae and the elegant Archaic *koroi* statues.

Thira Frescoes ②

The highly advanced settlement of Akrotiri, on the island of Thira (Santorini), was buried after a volcanic eruption in the 16th century BC. Beautiful frescoes, such as these boxer boys **(right)**, were perfectly preserved under the ash.

③ Archaic Koroi, 7th Century BC–480 BC

Koroi (statues of youths and maidens used at temples and graves) were the first monumental works in Greek art. The earliest are stiff and stylized, but through the 6th century the artists learnt to depict the body more naturalistically.

① Cycladic Collection, 3200–2200 BC

The Cycladic Museum *(see pp22–3)* has the largest collection from this civilization, but here you'll find some of the most unusual pieces, such as this harp-player **(above)**, showing, unusually, a three-dimensional figure in action.

Mycenaean Collection, 16th– ④ 11th Centuries BC

The Mycenaeans were famed both for their prowess as warriors and for the gold amassed by their traders. Parts of those hoards are displayed here, including the "Agamemnon" death mask **(right)** and priceless golden swords and jewellery.

⑤ Bronze Collection

This, the richest collection of bronze works from the Archaic and Classical eras, includes a majestic 460 BC sculpture of Poseidon or Zeus **(left)**, a 140 BC sculpture of a galloping horse and a youth of Antikythira.

6 Classical Statuary

The collection includes original marble sculptures from temples all around Greece. Highlights are those that adorned the Temple of Asklepios at Epidauros, works such as the 100 BC Diadoumenos and a marble copy of a late-5th-century bronze by the great sculptor Polykleitos.

7 Hellenistic Statuary

Here the stiff monuments of the Archaic period give way to sculptures that are full of vigorous movement and sensuality. This is especially so in the 100 BC group of Aphrodite, Pan and Eros, and the statue of a wounded Gaul.

8 Vases and Minor Art Collection

The collection contains impressive vases, terracotta figurines, gold jewels and glass vessels, dated from the 10th century BC up to the 18th century AD.

EARTHQUAKE

In September 1999, the strongest earthquake in a century rocked Athens, sending buildings tumbling and, in the National Archaeological Museum, shattering fragile pots. About half the museum was subsequently closed to the public, but reopened with all objects restored in 2004.

9 Grave Stelae

Classical marble grave sculptures **(below)** became so opulent by the end of the 4th century BC that they were banned. The scenes in these beautiful carvings typically show the deceased on the right, the bereaved on the left.

10 Egyptian Wing

This collection, from the Neolithic period to the end of the Roman era, is fascinating to view in conjunction with the earliest Greek Archaic art, which borrowed from Egyptian statuary before developing into its very own style. The collection includes a funerary boat sculpted from wood **(below)**.

NEED TO KNOW

MAP C1 ■ 44 Patision (28 Oktovriou)
■ 213 214 4800
■ www.namuseum.gr

Open May–Oct: 8am–8pm; Nov–Apr: 8am–3pm

Adm €15 (free first Sun of the month, Nov–Mar)

■ There's so much to see here that it makes sense to go twice – and to invest in one of the short informational guide books available at the museum.

■ There is an atrium café inside the museum and a larger café out the front.

TOP 10 ⭐ Museum of Cycladic Art

A delightful setting in which to ponder elegant, semi-abstract Cycladic figurines – remnants of a culture that flourished in the Cyclades from 3200–2000 BC. The beautiful marble carvings are unlike anything found in contemporary civilizations. Most are female forms – possibly cult objects of a goddess religion – and their elemental shapes have inspired many 20th-century artists.

1 Dove Vase

Carved entirely from one block of marble, this vase, decorated with doves (above), is the most remarkable of a series of vessels found in tombs. Archaeologists believe birds held an important meaning for the Cycladic culture, since they appear in many other carvings as well – but the nature of that significance remains to be established.

2 Red-Figure Column Krater

This vase (right), attributed to the Agrigento Painter, active in Attica in the 5th century BC, shows a girl musician playing a double flute and a young man holding a lyre. Between them is a dancing youth. The group is led by an ivy-wreathed boy carrying an amphora on his shoulders.

3 "Modigliani" Figure

So-called because the lines of this figure (left) show up clearly in the work of painter Amedeo Modigliani (1884–1920). The slender, simple shape, crossed arms and smooth face are all classic Cycladic traits. Non-standing feet indicate that such figures would probably have been lying down.

4 Female Figurine

The limestone female figurine has deep eye sockets and modelled breasts. It belongs to a group of human-form sculptures from the Chalcolithic period (3900–2500 BC).

5 Bronze Helmets

The Corinthian helmet underwent quite a development in the 7th century BC, with the shape being progressively altered in order to fit better on the head. It was the first helmet to be fashioned from a single bronze sheet, and it protected every part of the head (right).

THE GOULANDRIS DYNASTY

The founders of the Museum of Cycladic Art, the Goulandris family, are arguably Greece's greatest shipping dynasty (they had a long-standing rivalry with Onassis). They are also known for their love of the arts: in addition to this Athens museum, the Goulandris family also founded the Museum of Contemporary Art on the island of Andros.

6 Symposium Kylix

This exceptional piece of 5th-century BC pottery **(below)** shows a naked youth drawing wine from a large mixing vessel, known as a krater, to fill the cup he holds in his left hand. According to the inscription, the young man is named Lysis, and his beauty is praised by the addition of the epithet "fair".

Plan of the Museum of Cycladic Art

Key to Floorplan

- Cycladic Art
- Ancient Greek Art
- Ancient Cypriot Art
- Scenes from Daily Life in Antiquity

7 Dionysus Vase

This beautifully preserved 6th-century BC vase shows the god of wine and revelry Dionysus on one side (flanked by dancing satyrs) and, on the other side, Athena and Hermes conversing.

8 Male Figure

The only male figure of its size found so far in the prototypical Cycladic style. Attributed by some scholars to the Goulandris Master, who created the finest female figures, it has the same shape and placement of the arms. The separated legs indicate a standing pose, rather than the typically prone pose of the female figures.

9 Hunter-Warrior and Queen

The male and female figures, with elongated arms and almond-shaped eyes, are the most naturalistic of the later Cycladic figures. Experts believe that the dagger carved around the male figure indicates that he was a hunter-warrior.

NEED TO KNOW

MAP P3 ■ Neofytou Douka 4 and Vasilissis Sofias ■ 210 722 8321 ■ www.cycladic.gr

Open 10am–5pm Mon, Wed–Sun (to 8pm Thu, from 11am Sun); closed Tue

Adm €7 (€3.50 on Mon); concessions €2.50–€3.50

■ All the featured exhibits are found in the main building of the Cycladic Wing, while the Stathatos Mansion shows temporary exhibitions.

■ School and tour groups crowd the museum most mornings. If you can, leave your visit until after 1pm.

■ The museum's atrium café makes a great spot for a light lunch.

10 Stathatos Mansion

In 1991, the museum took over the adjoining Stathatos Mansion, a gilded Neo-Classical confection by Bavarian architect Ernst Ziller (see p102). Here the museum holds temporary exhibitions, receptions and lectures **(above)**.

TOP 10 ⭐ Roman Forum and Tower of the Winds

In the first century AD, the Romans moved Athens' marketplace here from the old Agora. Smaller than the original, the marble-pillared courtyard was a grander place to set up shop, and this became the city's commercial and administrative centre until the 19th century. Its greatest attraction was the unique and brilliantly designed Tower of the Winds.

3 Tower of the Winds

The octagonal tower (left), built by Syrian astronomer Andronikos Kyrrhestas in 50 BC, has personifications of the winds on each side. Inside, a water clock was operated by a stream from the Acropolis.

4 Fetiye Mosque

During the Ottoman occupation, the Forum remained an important cultural centre. In 1456, the Turks built this "Mosque of the Conqueror" directly over the ruins of an early Christian church.

1 Byzantine Grave Markers

In Byzantine times, when the Tower of the Winds was used as a church, the area around it was a cemetery. Graves were marked with cylindrical engraved markers, some of which were quite beautiful. These were later gathered in one place, along with others from around Athens.

2 Vespasianae (68-seat Public Latrine)

The pleasantly situated marble facility was housed in a rectangular building with a courtyard in the middle, and latrines lining all four sides. Proximity wasn't a problem – latrines were social gathering places.

5 Courtyard

This was the centre of activity. The courtyard was surrounded by shops and workshops selling food, cloth, ceramics, jewellery and wares from abroad. The Emperor Hadrian had the courtyard paved in the 2nd century AD.

6 Fountain

This splashing marble fountain (below), whose waters, like those of the water clock, may also have been sourced from the Acropolis, once provided cool relief to market-goers. But stay away from the brackish water that occasionally fills it today.

7 Gate of Athena Archegetis

The monumental four-columned western entrance to the forum **(left)** is built of beautiful Pentelic marble. It was built in 11 BC by Julius Caesar and Augustus, and dedicated by the people of Athens to the goddess Athena.

A MISCELLANY OF FINDS

Ever since the 1940s, archaeologists have used the forum as a repository for small, unclassifiable finds from all over Attica. Thus the site is studded with out-of-place but fascinating extras, such as the wall of mismatched capital pieces near the Vespasianae, and the garlanded sarcophagus, about which little is known, by the fountain.

Roman columns and the Fetiye Mosque behind

8 East Propylon

This is one of the two original entrances to the marketplace. In a stoa next to it are sculptures of important Romans, probably officials or emperors, which market-goers would have seen while coming and going.

9 Agoranomeion

This two-roomed building was believed, until recently, to be the office of market officials. Current theories say it may have been part of a cult to Claudius or Nero.

NEED TO KNOW

MAP J4–K4 ■ Aiolou and Diogenous, Monastiraki ■ 210 324 5220 ■ www.culture.gr

Open 8am–3pm daily. Times are subject to change; call ahead to confirm

Adm €6 (students half price), or included in €30 Acropolis ticket

■ During the harvest moon in late August (considered to be the biggest, brightest moon of the year), there is a free moonlit classical concert here.

■ Most restaurants around the Roman Forum are overpriced. Head to O Platanos taverna and enjoy delicious, authentic Greek dishes in a great atmosphere *(see p83)*.

Map of the Roman Forum

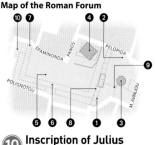

10 Inscription of Julius Caesar and Augustus

The inscription denoting that the Gate of Athena Archegetis was built by Caesar and Augustus is so faded that it can now only be seen at noon precisely. Stand outside the forum, and look directly at the top of the entrance.

TOP 10 ⭐ Benaki Museum

This vast museum gives a panoramic view of Greek history from the Stone Age (7000 BC) to the 20th century, by way of Classical Greece and the eras of the Byzantine and Ottoman empires. Over 20,000 objects are laid out in chronological order in 36 rooms, showing the evolution of Greek painting, sculpture and handicrafts.

1 Paintings by El Greco
Domenikos Theotokopoulos (1541–1614) became known as El Greco while living in Spain. Two early works here, completed while the artist was still in his native Crete, include *St Luke Painting the Virgin and Child* (left), painted around 1567.

2 Thebes Treasure
During the late Bronze Age, ornamental jewellery was used to display personal wealth. This hoard of Mycenaean gold jewellery includes an engraved gold signet ring, depicting a sacred marriage connected to the worship of a prehistoric goddess.

3 Thessaly Treasure
This stunning display of Hellenistic gold jewellery from the 3rd–2nd centuries BC employs filigree and granulation (beads of gold soldered onto metal) to produce minutely crafted earrings, necklaces, bracelets and diadems. One of the highlights is a decorative band with a knot of Herakles at its centre.

4 The Building
This Neo-Classical mansion of 1867 (above) was bought by Emmanuel Benakis in 1910, passed to his children, and then presented to the state in 1931 when it opened as a museum.

5 Mid-18th-Century Reception Room
The richly painted and gilded wooden ceiling and panelled walls of this room (below) – a reconstruction from a Macedonian mansion – recall a time when these crafts flourished locally.

6 Café
Cultural overload? Take a break on the rooftop terrace café overlooking the trees and lawns of the National Gardens.

NEED TO KNOW

MAP N3 ■ Koumpari 1, Kolonaki ■ 210 367 1000 ■ www.benaki.gr

Open 9am–5pm Wed & Fri, 9am–midnight Thu & Sat, 9am–3pm Sun ■ Closed Mon & Tue

Adm €9; students free; free Thu

■ Bear in mind that the museum has free admission and late-night opening every Thursday.

■ It is almost impossible to see the entire Benaki collection in one go: explore one section in the morning, stop for lunch in the rooftop café, then see the rest in the afternoon.

7 Evia Treasure
Around 3000 BC, the introduction of metallurgy marked the transition from the Stone Age to the Bronze Age. Outstanding examples from this period are three cups, two gold (below) and one silver, hammered into simple forms with minimal decoration. They date from between 3000 and 2800 BC.

8 A Second Room from Kozani
Another reconstruction from Macedonia, this mid-18th-century reception room features a minutely carved wooden ceiling, ornate built-in wooden cupboards and a low seating area, complete with Persian rugs and cushions, and a wrought-iron coffee table.

WHO WAS BENAKIS?

Antonis Benakis (1873–1954) was born in Egypt to an immensely wealthy merchant, Emmanuel Benakis, who later became Mayor of Athens. Antonis began collecting Islamic art while in Alexandria and went on to collect Byzantine art and Greek folk art once in Athens. He donated the entire collection to the Greek state in 1931. His sister, Penelope Delta (1874–1941), was a much-loved author of children's books.

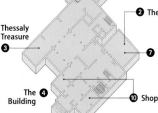

Café 6

Greek Independence Memorabilia 9

Mid-18th-Century Reception Room 5

Key to Floorplan
- Ground floor
- First floor
- Second floor
- Third floor

8 A Second Room from Kozani

1 Paintings by El Greco

2 Thebes Treasure

Thessaly Treasure 3

7 Evia Treasure

The Building 4

10 Shop

9 Greek Independence Memorabilia
Finely decorated swords, sabres and rifles, a painting of a freedom fighter from 1821, the flag of Hydra island (below) proclaiming "either victory or death", and a writing desk belonging to Lord Bryon are among the displays.

10 Shop
Here, exhibits such as ceramic bowls and tiles, jewellery and Byzantine icons have been carefully reproduced, using original craft techniques where possible.

Following pages View over Plaka towards Lykavittos Hill

TOP 10 ⭐ Kerameikos

Ancient Athens' outer walls run through Kerameikos, once the edge of the Classical city. Warriors and priestesses returned to Athens via two separate roads through here (one leading to a brothel, the other to a temple). Statesmen and heroes were buried beneath showy tombs lining the roads. But Kerameikos was also the scene of far shadier activities: the haunt of prostitutes, money-lenders and wine-sellers.

Pompeiion ①
The Pompeiion **(right)** was used to prepare for festive and religious processions, especially the annual Panathenaic procession, in which a new garment was brought to the statue of Athena in the Parthenon.

② City Walls
The walls, which surrounded the entire city, were built by Athenian ruler Themistockles in 478 BC. They incorporated materials from all over the city, including marble from tombs, temples and houses.

④ Dipylon
The main roads from Thebes, Corinth and the Peloponnese led to this entrance gate to Athens, the largest in ancient Greece. Many ceremonial events were held here to mark arrivals and departures.

⑤ Sanctuary of the Tritopatores
It is uncertain who exactly the Tritopatores were, but they may have been representatives of the souls of the dead, and worshipped in an ancestor cult.

Marble Bull ⑥
The bull of the tomb of Dionysios of Kollytos **(right)** is perhaps the most recognizable monument here. Its inscriptions tell us that Dionysios was praised for his goodness, and died unmarried, mourned by his mother and sisters.

③ Sacred Gate
Through this well-preserved gate **(above)** passed the Sacred Way, reserved for pilgrims and priestesses during the procession to Eleusis *(see p117)*. A great marble sphinx was built into the gate.

Plan of Kerameikos

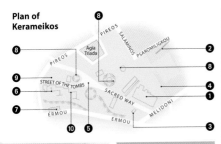

NEED TO KNOW

MAP A3–4

■ Ermou 148, Thissio
■ 210 346 3552

Open 8am–8pm daily.
Times are subject to
change; call ahead to
confirm

Adm: €8, or included
with €30 Acropolis ticket

Oberlander Museum:
8am–8pm daily. Times
are subject to change;
call ahead to confirm

■ The green site and
surrounding industrial
buildings are at their
most eerily lovely in the
early evening, when
they are tinged pink by
the setting sun.

■ There are several
reasonably priced
tavernas lining the
nearby streets of
Apostolou Pavlou and
Adrianou. Head to
either for a traditional
outdoor lunch.

**THE OLD POTTERS'
DISTRICT**

The name Kerameikos
comes from Keramos,
the patron god of
ceramics. According
to Pausanias (see p45)
and other early writers,
the name recalls an age-
old group of potters'
workshops that used
to be located on the
grassy banks of the
river Eridanos, which
cuts through the site.
The museum contains
fine examples of Greek
urns and other pottery
found at the site.

⑧ Warriors' Tombs

The high, round burial
mounds (tumuli) lining
the holy road date from
the 7th century BC and
were probably first built
to honour great warriors.
Most have marble coffins
and offerings at their
centres, with the mounds
built up around them.

⑨ Stele of Hegeso

This lovely grave
pediment is one of
the finest works of
5th-century BC Attic
art. Hegeso, the dead
woman, is portrayed
seated, taking a trinket
from a box. The original
is in the National
Archaeological Museum.

⑩ Tomb of Dexileos

This marble-relief carved
tomb (below) is of a
young horseman who
died in 394 BC. The dead
of ancient Greece were
often depicted along with
their living family, saying
a final goodbye.

⑦ Oberlander Museum

This small museum
(above) is packed with
fascinating finds, such as
originals of many tombs
replaced by casts and
pottery shards of erotic
scenes from a brothel.

TOP 10 ⭐ Byzantine and Christian Museum

From c. AD 330 to 1453, the Byzantine Empire dominated the Mediterranean region. The wealthy Orthodox Church was the most important influence in Byzantium, and left behind a vast legacy. This collection embraces 15,000 objects taken from that period.

1 Shepherd Carrying a Lamb

This 4th-century marble sculpture is also a Christian allegory with pagan roots. Though the shepherd is meant to be Christ, the image is taken directly from an Archaic sculpture found on the Acropolis of a man bringing a calf to be slaughtered to the goddess Athena.

2 Treasury of Mytilene

A collection of 6th-century silver vessels, gold jewellery and coins, discovered in a sunken ship off the island of Mytilene (Lesvos). Scholars believe the valuables were brought to the island to be hidden, and were never recovered by their owners.

3 Orpheus Playing a Lyre

Orpheus (left) is surrounded by animals, creating an allegory of Christ and his followers. This transmutation of ancient pagan myths into the new religion of Christianity was an essential element of Byzantine art.

5 Mosaic Icon of the Virgin (The Episkepsis)

This 13th-century mosaic (above) shows the Virgin and Child, with a gold background symbolizing divine light. Mosaic icons are very rare – only about 40 are known to exist, all of which, like this one, originate from Constantinople.

4 Precious Ecclesiastical Artifacts

This case contains a late 14th-century wooden cross covered with silver and embellished with small steatite icons, a 10th-century copper chalice, and a 14th-century silk stole decorated with holy figures embroidered in metallic and silk thread.

NEED TO KNOW

MAP P3 ▪ Vasilissis Sofias 22 ▪ 213 213 9500 ▪ www.byzantine museum.gr

Open 8am–8pm daily. Times are subject to change, call ahead to confirm

Adm €8; students €4; under 18s free

▪ In summer, there are often concerts in the courtyard. Call ahead to find out what's on and when.

▪ There is a café-bistro located in the museum garden. Alternatively, head to one of the cafés or restaurants on Plateia Kolonaki.

8 Double-Sided Icon of St George

Large, double-sided icons were extremely rare in Byzantium. This 13th-century example **(left)** is especially unusual, as it is carved in three dimensions and depicts the full body.

ARISTOTLE'S LYCEUM

Building plans for the neighbouring site were shelved when some ancient ruins were discovered. These were later identified as the Lyceum of Aristotle (the school that the philosopher founded to compete with Plato's Academy). The site has been taken over by the museum.

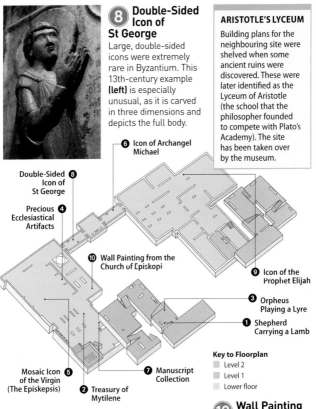

6 Icon of Archangel Michael

8 Double-Sided Icon of St George

4 Precious Ecclesiastical Artifacts

10 Wall Painting from the Church of Episkopi

9 Icon of the Prophet Elijah

3 Orpheus Playing a Lyre

1 Shepherd Carrying a Lamb

Key to Floorplan
- Level 2
- Level 1
- Lower floor

5 Mosaic Icon of the Virgin (The Episkepsis)

7 Manuscript Collection

2 Treasury of Mytilene

6 Icon of Archangel Michael

Set in a glowing field of gold, this 14th-century icon from Constantinople, Turkey, depicts the Archangel Michael with a sceptre and orb, symbolic of the terrestrial world.

7 Manuscript Collection

The highlight of this collection is a 14th-century imperial document issued by Emperor Andronicus II. The top of the scroll bears a miniature showing the emperor himself handing a document to Christ, while at the bottom, the emperor's signature appears in red ink.

9 Icon of the Prophet Elijah

This 17th-century icon, fully titled *The Ascension of the Prophet Elijah and Scenes from his Life* is signed by Cretan artist Theodore Poulakis. It depicts the prophet riding a golden chariot pulled by four red horses, a scene inspiring an earlier engraving by the Flemish print-maker Jan Wierix.

10 Wall Painting from the Church of Episkopi

Created between the 10th and 13th centuries, these paintings **(below)** depict biblical scenes in muted hues. They are displayed in the position they would have had in the church, which was based on a "cross in square" plan with a dome and Narthex.

TOP10 ⭐ Filopappos Hill

The pine-covered slopes of Filopappos Hill offer a pleasantly shaded maze of paths leading through monuments marking centuries of history. Known as "the hill of muses" in antiquity, it has been a source of inspiration for countless poets. On the first day of Lent, the hill is swarmed with hundreds of Athenians, who gather here to fly kites.

4 Socrates' Prison

This is believed to be the cave **(left)** where Socrates *(see p44)* was imprisoned, having been condemned to death. His disciples sat with him as he drank the hemlock that dispatched him.

1 The Deme of Koile

This ancient road leads from the Acropolis to Piraeus, passing between Filopappos Hill and the Pnyx to follow the course of the Long Walls (5th century BC). It was a two-lane road, 8–12 m (26–40 ft) wide, with anti-slip grooves. A 500-m (1,600-ft) stretch has been excavated.

5 The Pnyx

If Athens is the cradle of democracy, this spot **(right)** is its exact birthplace. After Athens became a democracy in 508 BC, the first ever democratic congress met here weekly, and the greatest orators held forth. The limestone theatre, cut into the hill, accommodated over 10,000.

2 Old National Observatory

Greece's oldest research centre is housed in a beautiful Neo-Classical building. The centre monitors astronomy, weather and, especially, the earthquakes that occasionally rattle Athens.

6 Church of Agia Marina

Agia Marina **(below)** is associated with childbirth and sick children, and so pregnant women come here and slip down a carved slide to ensure a safe delivery. In the past, mothers brought sick children here to spend the night. A colourful festival honours Marina each July.

7 Church of Agios Dimitrios Loumbardiaris

In 1648, an Ottoman commander planned to bombard this charming Byzantine church. But lightning struck his cannon, giving the church the name of "St Dimitri the Bombadier".

3 Hill of the Nymphs

In ancient times, Greeks believed Filopappos was inhabited by the muses of art, music and poetry. This smaller hill was the home of the nymphs – the female spirits of trees and springs.

8 Filopappos Monument

Roman senator Gaius Julius Antiochus Filopappos was a lover of Classical Greek culture. He took his retirement in Athens and died here in about AD 114. The Greeks built this marble tomb and monument to the senator **(left)**, showing him as an Athenian citizen, surrounded by his royal Roman family. Its partially destroyed form looks across to the Acropolis.

THE 1687 SIEGE

During an attempt to seize the Ottoman-occupied Acropolis, the Venetians garrisoned themselves on Filopappos Hill, the perfect strategic location to shell their target. Too perfect, unfortunately – one of their shells hit the Parthenon, where the Turks stored their gunpowder, and the ensuing explosion severely damaged the Acropolis's prized temple and sculptures.

9 Hilltop View

You may not feel that you deserve such a jaw dropping view after such an easy, shaded walk. But the hilltop directly overlooks the Acropolis and all of southern Athens stretching to the sea. This was once a favourite vantage-point for generals – and it's equally appealing to photographers today.

NEED TO KNOW

MAP B6 ■ Enter from Dionysiou Areopagitou ■ www.culture.gr

Dora Stratou Dance Theatre:
MAP C5 ■ Performances late May–late Sep: 9:30pm Wed–Fri, 8:15pm Sat–Sun, call to confirm. Tickets from the theatre, or call 210 324 4395

■ Though perfectly safe during the day, the unlit paths of Filopappos Hill are best avoided after dark.

■ There is a pleasant café called the Loumbardiaris among the trees just behind the Church of Agios Dimitrios Loumbardiaris. Stop here for refreshments and food before walking up to the top of the hill.

10 Dora Stratou Dance Theatre

Dora Stratou's troupe travels the land, learning and keeping alive hundreds of regional dances. Here, they present the intricate moves that have been part of Greek culture for centuries.

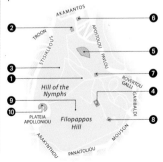

TOP 10 ⭐ Temple of Olympian Zeus

The majestic temple to the ruler of the pantheon was the largest on mainland Greece. Inside stood two colossal gold and ivory statues: one of the god, and one of the Roman Emperor Hadrian. Though the temple's construction began in 515 BC, political turmoil delayed its completion for nearly 700 years. To thank Hadrian for finishing it, in AD 131 the Athenians built a two-storey arch next to the temple, whose inscription announces Hadrian's claim on the city.

1 Valerian Wall
Enclosing several buildings within the temple complex was a wall **(below)** commissioned by the Roman emperor Valerian in the 3rd century AD. Many of the temples it surrounded were demolished to provide marble for the wall.

WHY DID IT TAKE SO LONG TO BUILD?

The tyrant Peisistratos started the Temple of Olympian Zeus in 515 BC to keep the rebellious Athenians occupied. After his fall, the democratic Athenians refused to finish what they saw as a monument to a hated tyrant. In 174 BC, King Antiochus IV of Epiphanes took over the construction work, but it stopped with his death in 163 BC. When Hadrian arrived in AD 124, he ordered the temple to be completed.

2 Temple of Olympian Zeus
Zeus had long been worshipped on this site, and there was at least one other temple to him before this one. Sixteen magnificent columns **(above)** survive from the original 104.

3 Hadrian's Arch
Emperor Hadrian had the west side of this arch **(right)** inscribed "This is Athens, the ancient city of Theseus", and the east side "This is the city of Hadrian and not of Theseus", distinguishing the cities of ancient legend and modern reality.

4 **Themistoklean Gates**

Around the site are remains of the wall built by political leader Themistokles in 479 BC, to defend Athens from continuing onslaughts by the Persians.

5 **Law Court at the Delphinion**

Now mostly in ruins, this law court, from 500 BC, is thought to be on the site of the palace of mythical king Aegeus, the father of Theseus (see p47).

6 **Roman Baths**

Among the many ruins of "Hadrianopolis", the first structures of Hadrian's new city, are these foundations (above), actually the best-preserved Roman bath house in Athens. It once had a coloured mosaic floor.

7 **Temple of Apollo Delphinios and Artemis Delphinia**

The temple was built to honour the god-and-goddess siblings Apollo and Artemis, celebrating them in the form of two dolphins.

NEED TO KNOW

MAP L5 ■ Leoforos Vas. Olgas 1 at Amalias
■ 210 922 6330
■ www.culture.gr

Open 8am–8pm daily. Times are subject to change; call to confirm

Adm €6, or included with €30 Acropolis ticket

....

■ To get the best light for photographs of the column capitals, come between 3 and 4pm.

■ For a bite to eat, head across the street to Zappeion Gardens to either the elegant Aigli café and restaurant or one of the other cafés spread through the park.

8 **Ruins of Houses**

Ancient pipes, foundations and domestic objects show that people lived and built houses here between the 5th century BC and 2nd century AD – the whole time it took to build the temple.

9 **Temple of Kronos and Rhea**

This temple to Zeus's parents was built in the 5th century BC; now only the foundations remain. Rhea saved Zeus from Kronos, then Zeus took dominion of the universe as ruler of the gods.

10 **Temple of Zeus Panhellenios**

Hadrian promoted the cult of Zeus Panhellenios ("ruler of all the Greeks") and associated himself with the god. Offers to god and emperor were made in this temple, later demolished for the Valerian wall.

Map of the Temple Site

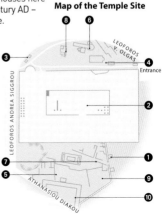

The Top 10
of Everything

**Archaeological display at the
Acropolis Museum, Athens**

Moments in History

① Birth of Athens
The Acropolis was first inhabited in Neolithic times (around 3000 BC), and began to take on the form of a city when it was fortified by the Mycenaeans (inhabitants of the southeastern Greek mainland) in about 1400 BC.

② Golden Age
The 6th and 5th centuries BC saw the city-state develop into a colonial power. Under Perikles (495–429 BC) Athens enjoyed its greatest period of building, when the Parthenon, Erechtheion and Temple of Nike were erected. Cultural life flourished until Sparta's defeat of Athens in the Peloponnesian War (431–404 BC).

Bust of the Greek statesman Perikles

③ Roman Athens
Roman rule began in 146 BC and lasted five centuries. Athenians initially maintained good relations with their rulers, but in 86 BC a move towards independence was brutally crushed by the Romans. Emperor Hadrian (AD 76–138) remained a great admirer of Greek culture, however, and, together with

Greek scholar Herodes Atticus, he set up various building schemes, including the great theatre *(see p13)*.

④ Byzantine Period
In AD 395, when Roman territory was divided between East and West, Greece fell within the East, later becoming part of the Byzantine Empire. The pagan philosophical schools were closed and many temples were rebuilt as churches.

⑤ The Ottomans Take Athens
The Ottoman Turks took Athens in 1458, and the city became a provincial backwater. After bombarding the Parthenon, the Venetians held the city briefly in 1687. In the 1700s, English and French artists visited Athens as part of the Grand Tour, contributing to its rebirth, but also walking off with many ancient artworks.

⑥ War of Independence
In 1821 Greeks rose up against Ottoman domination – initially alone, then with the aid of Britain, France and Russia. The war ended in 1829, but the Ottomans held the Acropolis until 1834, when King Otto I entered the city. Athens became capital of the new Greek state and was rebuilt, largely in Neo-Classical style.

Painting of the War of Independence

(7) World War II

Mussolini declared war on Greece in October 1940, and the German army entered Athens in April 1941, raising the swastika over the Acropolis. The Third Reich used the Hotel Grande Bretagne (see p144) as its wartime headquarters.

German planes during World War II

(8) Post World War II

At the close of WWII, with its political future uncertain, Greece fell into civil war. The US began pouring economic and military aid into the country, on the proviso that the Communist Left would not gain power. In the 1950s and '60s, Athens saw rapid industrialization, mass migration from rural areas and the growth of sprawling suburbs.

(9) Military Dictatorship

In April 1967, a coup d'état led by Georgios Papadopoulos signalled the beginning of a seven-year military junta. Student protests on 17 November 1973 were violently suppressed by the military, who stormed Athens' Polytechnic and killed many. The regime fell in 1974.

(10) Modern-Day Athens

Greece joined the EEC (now the EU) in 1981. In 1985, Athens was the first European City of Culture. The successful 2004 Olympics left the city with improved transport, sports and cultural facilities. However, since 2011 the economic crisis has delivered harsh austerity, leading to public protests in Athens and snap elections. Greece continues to debate its membership of the EU.

TOP 10 ATHENIANS

1 Athena
In Ancient Greek mythology, Athena (see also pp46–7) became the patron of Athens.

2 Theseus
Legendary king who embodied the qualities of youth, beauty, intelligence, good fortune and heroism.

3 Draco
In the 7th century BC, Draco instituted the first Code of Law: even trivial crimes incurred the death penalty, hence the term draconian.

4 Solon
Draco's laws were made less severe by Solon (c.638–559 BC). He also extended citizenship to the lower classes.

5 Cleisthenes
Statesman of around 570–507 BC, who replaced the rule of the aristocracy with a democratic Assembly.

6 Themistokles
This general (c.524–460 BC) championed the navy as a force to expand the empire.

7 Perikles
Perikles (c.495–429 BC) beautified the city, let poorer citizens attend the Assembly, and extended the empire.

8 Aspasia
In the 5th century BC, this courtesan gained acceptance in Athens' male-dominated intellectual circles.

9 Demosthenes
The finest Greek orator (384–322 BC) overcame a speech impediment by talking with pebbles in his mouth.

10 Melina Mercouri
Much-loved actress (1920–94) who opposed the 1967–74 junta, became Minister of Culture and initiated the European City of Culture scheme.

The actress Melina Mercouri

TOP 10 Moments in the History of Theatre and Music

A modern production of *The Persians*, a play by Aeschylus

1 The Rites of Dionysus, 1200–600 BC

Annual rites to the god of wine and revelry were held each spring, and involved orgies, feasts and the ingestion of herbs that led to wild ecstasies. A dithyramb (ode to Dionysus) was sung by a chorus of men dressed as satyrs. It eventually evolved into narratives, which in turn developed into the first plays.

2 Thespis, 6th Century BC

During one of these group chorales, an intrepid performer named Thespis broke away from the group and added a solo narrative. The innovation took hold, and this new individual role became known as the protagonist, the individual hero of the drama, now backed by the chorus.

3 Drama Competitions, 534 BC

In 534 BC, the ruler of Athens, Pisistratus, formalized the Dionysian festivals into fully fledged drama competitions, held annually. Thespis won the first competition.

4 Aeschylus, the First Playwright, 472 BC

Aeschylus introduced a second character, the antagonist, creating new possibilities. In 472 BC came *Persians*, the earliest known play.

5 Sophocles Beats Aeschylus in the Drama Competition, 468 BC

Sophocles brought another innovation to the form of drama: a third character. He also wrote what is still considered the greatest masterpiece of tragedy, *Oedipus Rex*.

6 Greek Shadow Puppet Theatre, 16th Century

After the Golden Age of Athenian drama, Greece's performing arts stagnated. However, during the Turkish occupation, Greeks drew on an Eastern tradition of shadow puppet theatre. The stylized spectacles were satirical and bawdy, the main character (Karaghiozis the fool) joking at the expense of his Turkish masters.

Greek shadow puppet

7 Rembetika Emerges, 1870s

When the Greeks threw off 400 years of Turkish occupation, one of the first art forms to coalesce was rembetika, music that can be compared to the blues. Heavily influenced by music and instruments from Asia Minor, rembetika lyrics tell of life's underside: drugs, destitution, passion, lust and squalor.

8 Maria Callas Dominates Opera, 1950s and 1960s

Born Maria Kalogeropoulos, the fiery first lady of opera was the original diva. She enraged many opera house managers with her whims, but she also seduced millions, including shipping magnate Aristotle Onassis, with her heavenly voice.

9 Mikis Theodorakis Writes the Songs of a Generation, 1960s and 1970s

Mikis Theodorakis, Greece's greatest modern composer, won international acclaim with works such as *Epiphania* and the instantly recognizable *Zorba the Greek* score. During the junta, Theodorakis's songs were banned and he was jailed, making him an instant symbol of the resistance.

A scene from *Chariots of Fire*

10 Vangelis's Chariots of Fire, 1981

Greek composer Vangelis won an Academy Award for his memorable score for *Chariots of Fire*, a film about Olympic runners. Vangelis is renowned for his electronic compositions and film scores, and retains superstar status in Greece.

TOP 10 VENUES

Odeon of Herodes Atticus

1 Odeon of Herodes Atticus
Entrance: MAP J5 ▪ Dionysiou Areopagitou ▪ 210 324 1807 ▪ Box office: MAP L/M2 ▪ Panepistimiou 39
This huge amphitheatre was Athens' premiere showcase for performing arts for nearly 2,000 years (see p13).

2 Stoa Athanaton
Athens' favourite rembetatiko (see p99).

3 National Opera
A little moth-eaten, but this place is still loved by Athenians (see p96).

4 National Theatre
Home of the Greek National Theatre Company, whose performances of the classics are renowned (see p96).

5 An Club
Rock, reggae and alternative music in the heart of Exarcheia (see p99).

6 Gagarin
MAP B1 ▪ Liosion 205, Attiki ▪ 213 024 8358
Great musicians often play at this venue.

7 Megaro Mousikis
MAP G3 ▪ Vas Sofias and Kokkali ▪ 210 728 2000 ▪ Closed in summer
Fabulous acoustics for the world's best orchestras, ballets and opera companies.

8 Lykavittos Theatre
Open-air hillside theatre showcasing top-notch musical acts, from rock to classical (see p102).

9 Half Note
MAP M6 ▪ 210 921 3360/3310 ▪ Trivonianou 17
Every top jazz musician passing through Athens has played here.

10 Epidauros
Tickets available from the Herodes Atticus box office
Only ancient classics are performed in this famous amphitheatre (see p125).

Philosophers and Writers

1 Homer c.700 BC

Next to nothing is known about the bard who compiled the tales of *The Iliad* and *The Odyssey*. These poems, which were kept alive by oral tradition, are arguably the greatest and most influential in history.

2 Aeschylus 535–456 BC

When the "Father of Tragedy" began writing, theatre was still in its infancy. Aeschylus brought a wealth of characters, powerful narratives, grandeur of language, and a sweeping vision of humans working out a plan of cosmic justice to works such as *Prometheus Unbound* and acclaimed trilogy *The Oresteia*.

3 Sophocles 496–406 BC

Only seven of Sophocles' plays survive, but his reputation rests securely on three: *Antigone*, *Oedipus at Colonus* and *Oedipus Rex*. The last of these, the story of a king bound hopelessly by fate to murder his father and marry his mother, is considered the greatest masterpiece of Greek tragedy.

4 Socrates 470–399 BC

Though Socrates himself wrote nothing, his teachings, recorded in the writings of historians and especially his pupil Plato, have earned him the title of the forerunner of Western philosophy. At the height of the Golden Age of Athens, the original marketplace philosopher debated the great meanings in the Agora, and was eventually tried and put to death for corrupting the Athenian youth (see p34).

5 Aristophanes 447–385 BC

The greatest comic playwright of Greece brought a welcome breath of fresh air and levity after the age of the great tragedians. Aristophanes' raunchy, hilarious *Lysistrata*, in which the women of warring Sparta and Athens refuse to sleep with their husbands until they stop fighting, remains one of the greatest anti-war messages of all time.

Homer

6 Plato 428–348 BC

If Socrates was the forerunner of Western philosophy, then Plato was its foundation. His works – from his early dialogues reprising Socrates' teachings, to later masterworks such as the seminal *Republic* – comprised the backbone of every major intellectual movement to follow.

Plato and Aristotle, as portrayed by Raphael in *The School of Athens*

7 Aristotle 384–322 BC

After studying with Plato, Aristotle tutored Alexander the Great. He later set up the Lyceum, a competitor to Plato's Academy. His *Poetics* is still one of the most

Aristotle tutoring Alexander the Great

important works of literary criticism, and his *Nichomachean Ethics* is among the greatest treatises on ethics.

 Nikos Kazantzakis 1883–1957

Millions have been drawn to the strange, joyous, bittersweet spirit of modern Greece, as depicted in Kazantzakis' most famous work, *Zorba the Greek*. Darker in mood is *The Last Temptation of Christ*, and best of all is his audacious continuation of the fundamental Greek tale: *The Odyssey: A Modern Sequel*.

9 George Seferis 1900–71

Greece's first Nobel Laureate was born in Smyrna, which was later claimed by Turkey, and his lyrical poetry is inspired by history and feelings of exile. His work also relates Greece's Classical past to its raw present, as in *Mythistorema*, a series of poems that draws from *The Odyssey*.

10 Yanis Varoufakis b.1961

Challenging EU austerity measures while serving as Finance Minister in the left-wing Syriza government in 2015, Varoufakis stood out for being outspoken. This academic, political economist and game-theory expert remains a figure to watch in European politics.

TOP 10 TOMES

1 *The Iliad*, Homer
One small episode in the Trojan War, told in the greatest epic ever written.

2 *The Odyssey*, Homer
Detailing Odysseus's adventures with sirens, nymphs and Cyclops as he makes his way from Troy back home to the island of Ithaca.

3 *The Oresteia*, Aeschylus
Brilliant trilogy about the House of Atreus, the most dysfunctional family in ancient Greece.

4 *The Theban Tragedies*, Sophocles
Terrible events unfold when Oedipus kills his father and marries his mother. A dramatic text to read on a visit to Delphi and Thebes.

5 *The Republic*, Plato
Still the blueprint for the best way to run a government.

6 *Constitution of Athens*, Aristotle
A work that marries the democratic political structure of Athens with the architectural structure of the Agora.

7 *History of the Peloponnesian War*, Thucydides
Month-by-month, blow-by-blow historical account of the conflict by an Athenian officer.

8 *The Histories*, Herodotus
Compelling reportage of the Greeks' fight for freedom against the Persians, as told by the "Father of History".

9 *The Guide to Greece*, Pausanias
Pausanias, arguably the world's first travel writer, recorded observations from all over Greece during his 2nd-century journey.

10 *Zorba the Greek*, Nikos Kazantzakis
The quintessential modern Greek novel; a film was made in 1964.

Anthony Quinn in *Zorba the Greek*

TOP 10 Athenian Legends

Painting depicting the story of Theseus killing the Minotaur

1 Theseus Kills the Minotaur

After a dispute between Aegeus, King of Athens, and his brother Minos, King of Crete, Minos demanded Athens send regular tributes of 14 youths and maidens, who were sacrificed to the monstrous Minotaur. One year, Theseus asked to be sent and, with the help of Minos's daughter, Ariadne, he killed the Minotaur, saving hundreds of future Athenians.

2 The Birth of Erichtonius

Hephaestus tried to rape Athena, but only managed to spill his seed on her leg. Athena brushed it to the ground, where it grew into the baby Erichtonius ("earth-born"). Athena raised him to become a king, and he is considered the first ancestor of all Athenians.

The Birth of Erichtonius

3 The Birth of Athena

Zeus was told that his pregnant mistress Metis would have a son who would dethrone him. To prevent this, he swallowed Metis whole, but the unborn child continued to grow in Zeus's head. After nine months, Hephaestus split open the god's head with an axe, and out sprang the girl goddess Athena, in full armour.

4 The Naming of Athens

Athena and Poseidon, god of the sea, competed for patronage of the city by offering their best gifts. Poseidon struck his trident into the rock of the Acropolis and out gushed salt water. Athena offered the olive tree, and the city was awarded to her.

5 Theseus's Arrival in Athens

Theseus, son of King Aegeus, was raised far from court. At 16, wielding his father's sword, Theseus left for Athens, en route slaying dozens of monsters terrorizing Attica. He became Athens' greatest king.

6 The Rape of Philomela

Pandion had two daughters, Procne and Philomela. When the former's husband Tereus raped Philomela and cut out her tongue, Procne took revenge by serving the flesh of their son to Tereus. The gods then made Philomela into a swallow, Tereus into a hoopoe and Procne into a nightingale (which cries "Tereu").

7 The Trial of Orestes

After murdering his mother, Klytemnestra (to avenge her murder of his father, Agamemnon), Orestes was pursued to Athens by the Furies (goddesses of vengeance). Athena decreed that, instead of being killed, Orestes should stand trial. The trial marked a turning point in Athens, from blood feuds to rule of law.

8 Athena and Arachne

As goddess of spinning, Athena decided to help a poor but talented weaver called Arachne. Arachne won great admiration but never credited the goddess, so Athena challenged her to a weaving contest. Arachne's work depicted the inappropriate love affairs of the gods; Athena, furious with indignation, turned Arachne into the first spider.

Athena and Arachne

9 The Death of Aegeus

Theseus had told his father that if he succeeded in killing the Minotaur, he would change his ship's sails from black to white. But, after all the excitement, he forgot. Upon seeing the black sails, Aegeus was stricken with grief and plunged to his death in the sea (now the Aegean).

10 Perseus Kills Medusa

Perseus was the son of Zeus and the maiden Danae. The tyrant Polydectes desired Danae, but Perseus promised him the snake-infested head of Medusa in exchange for his mother's safety. Perseus slew Medusa with Athena's help, then he turned Polydectes to stone.

TOP 10 GODS AND MONSTERS

1 Zeus
The Pantheon's supreme god ruled the skies and fathered hundreds of heroes with his supernatural libido.

2 Poseidon
The god of the sea was Zeus's brother – and sometimes his greatest rival.

3 Athena
Zeus's daughter was a virgin warrior goddess of wisdom and philosophy. She was also goddess of weaving and patron of Athens.

4 Apollo
The handsome god of music and poetry presided over the Muses.

5 Artemis
Apollo's twin sister was goddess of the moon, wild animals and the hunt, and remained a virgin.

6 Aphrodite
Voluptuous Aphrodite was Artemis's polar opposite – the temperamental goddess of love had dozens of affairs.

7 The Minotaur
Crete's Queen Pasiphae conceived this bull-headed, human-bodied monster with a bull sent by Poseidon.

8 The Cyclops
The most famous of these one-eyed giants is Polyphemus, the monster son of Poseidon who Odysseus blinded in Homer's *The Odyssey*.

9 The Sirens
The beautiful sirens with their bewitching songs nearly lured Odysseus's sailors to their deaths on a rocky shore.

10 Medusa
The gaze of this snake-headed gorgon turned men to stone. Perseus defeated her only with the help of Athena's gleaming shield, in which he could safely see his foe.

Statue of the god Apollo

📊10 Greek Inventions

1 Olympic Games

The first recorded games were staged on the plains of Olympia in 776 BC. Dedicated to Zeus, they lasted one day and featured running and wrestling. In 472 BC – with the addition of boxing, the pancration (another form of hand-to-hand combat), horse racing and the pentathlon (sprinting, long-jump, javelin, discus and wrestling) – the event was extended to five days and held every four years.

The archaeological site at Olympia

2 Athenian Trireme

Masterpieces of ancient shipbuilding (c.700–500 BC), triremes were the key to Athens' naval strength. Approximately 40 m (130 ft) long and 5 m (15 ft) wide, they were noted for great speed – up to 12 knots. The boats were powered by 170 oarsmen seated on three tiers. Only one tier rowed at a time, alternating short shifts so that they did not exhaust themselves all at once. The vessels were also equipped with sails, which were lowered during battle.

3 Democracy

Demokratia ("power to the people") as a form of government was first introduced in Athens under Cleisthenes (570–507 BC). All free, male, adult citizens of Athenian birth were entitled to attend the Assembly – which met on the Pnyx Hill – and thus participate in political decision-making. The Assembly gathered about 40 times a year, and 6,000 citizens needed to be present to make a vote valid.

4 Pythagoras's Theorem

"The square of the hypotenuse of a right-angled triangle is equal to the sum of the squares of the other two sides." This theorem, discovered by the philosopher and mathematician Pythagoras (580–500 BC) was a major scientific breakthrough, which led to extraordinary advances in mathematics, geometry and astronomy.

5 Catapult

Invented by Dionysius the Elder of Syracuse (430–367 BC), the catapult can hurl heavy objects or shoot arrows over large distances. Having seized power in Sicily, Dionysius set about driving out the Carthaginians, who ruled a large part of the island. Thanks in part to the catapult, he was successful, making Syracuse the strongest power in Greek Italy. The Romans later perfected his invention, adding wheels to catapults to make them mobile.

6 Greek Fire

This was the secret weapon of the Byzantine Empire, used against enemy ships. Greek Fire was a highly flammable, jelly-like substance, which was blasted through bronze tubes mounted on the prows of Byzantine galleys, and could not be extinguished by water. It was first employed to repel an Arab fleet attacking Constantinople in 673, and then successfully used in combat until the Empire's fall in 1453. To this day scientists are unsure of its exact formula but think that it probably consisted of liquid petroleum, sulphur, naphtha and quicklime.

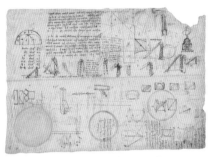

Leonardo da Vinci's sketch of Archimedes' Screw

with any patient, and to keep any information divulged to them confidential. The oath was taken by doctors until 1948, when the World Medical Association (considering references to ancient Greek myths somewhat obsolete) produced a modern restatement called the Declaration of Geneva.

7 Archimedes' Screw

The Syracusan-born Greek mathematician Archimedes (287–212 BC) invented an ingenious water pump, which became known as Archimedes' screw. It consisted of a tube coiled around a rod, which is set at an angle, with the bottom end in water and a handle at the top. When the handle is rotated, the entire device turns and the tube collects water which is thus transported upwards.

8 Hippocratic Oath

Attributed to the founding father of medicine, the Greek physician Hippocrates (460–375 BC), this oath prohibits doctors from performing abortions, euthanasia or unnecessary surgery, and requires them to abstain from sexual relations

9 Pap Smear

Since 1943, cervical cancer has been detected using the Pap smear test, a gynaecological procedure named after its inventor, the Athens-educated Greek-American doctor, George Papanicolaou (1883–1962).

10 Theatre

The earliest form of theatre can be traced back to an ancient Greek pagan ritual, which developed into an annual drama competition in the 6th century BC (see p42). Plays were performed outside in daylight in purpose-built amphitheatres, and actors wore a range of masks to indicate different characters. The oldest plays emphasize values such as Greek patriotism, reverence to the gods, liberty and hospitality.

The Theatre of Dyonisus Eleuthereus, Athens

🔟 Artistic Styles

1 Cycladic, 3200–2000 BC

The prehistoric Cycladic civilization flourished on the islands of Naxos, Paros, Amorgos, Santorini and Keros (which form a rough circle in the Aegean, hence the name) for 1,000 years, before mysteriously disappearing. It left behind hundreds of marble figures: most are elegant, angular, minimalist female figures, probably used in a goddess or fertility cult.

Angular Cycladic figurine

2 Minoan, 2000–1400 BC

The Minoans of Crete were sensual, social, nature-loving and matriarchal. Ceramics are painted with flowing lines based on natural motifs. Fluid-lined frescoes depict priestesses and animals. Most exciting are the faïence sculptures of voluptuous goddesses wielding snakes, and the fantastically light, delicate gold jewellery.

3 Mycenaean, 1500–1300 BC

The art of this martial mainland culture was somewhat influenced by the Minoans. But they were fundamentally different, focused on war, order and acquisition, especially of gold. Their palaces housed hoards of embossed-gold swords, daggers, and cups, gold death-masks and pots painted with warrior images.

4 Geometric, 8th–7th Century BC

Geometric art emerged from a dark age with vases painted with angular designs, and abstract, triangular-rectilinear human forms. The greatest of these is the giant 8th-century BC funerary vase in the National Archaeological Museum, where you can also see the first "Greek key" pattern.

Admiring archaic sculptures

5 Archaic, Late 7th–5th Century BC

The start of monumental Greek art, with the first marble temples and sculptures. Early statues of young men and women, called *koroi*, and made for religious purposes, were heavily influenced by Egyptian art: stiff, still, with garments and facial features carved and brightly painted.

6 Classical, 500–320 BC

The advent of naturalistic sculptures balancing vibrancy and idealism. Temples were built according to mathematical proportions, adorned with tradition-shattering sculptural reliefs that seemed to break out from the marble. Many were created by the sculptor Pheidias, a central figure of Athens' Golden Age.

Reconstructed Mycenaean mosaic

7 Hellenistic, 320 BC–1st Century AD

Classical sculpture grew ripe and decadent, in part influenced by the new Hellenistic cities in the Orient, part of Alexander the Great's empire. The sculptor Lysippos defined the new phase with sensuous subjects such as Aphrodite, Pan and Dionysus in exaggerated, twisting movement.

14th-century Byzantine icon

8 Byzantine, c. 330–1453

Byzantine art was almost completely focused on depicting Christian images. Rich, colourful mosaics, frescoes, icons and religious objects were made with valuable materials, especially gold, and using intricate methods, which conveyed the wealth of the empire.

9 Ottoman Influence, 1453–1821

Under the Turks, cultural activities and art were stifled, but folk arts persisted, incorporating some aspects from the conqueror's culture, including intricate silver jewellery and metalwork and colourful rugs, tapestries and embroideries.

10 Neo-Classical, 1821– Early 20th Century

After defeating their Ottoman conquerors, the Greeks began rebuilding the country, turning to the well-proportioned forms of their Classical forebears. Many of modern Athens' most important buildings were constructed on this model, notably the University of Athens, the Academy of Athens and the National Library.

TOP 10 ARTISTIC TERMS

1 Kouros/Kore
The first monumental sculptures in Greek art: a *kouros* was a youth, a *kore* a maiden. The plural is *koroi*.

2 Capital
The top of a column. There are three main Greek forms: Doric, a simple slab; Ionic, a carved scroll; and Corinthian, with an acanthus-leaf pattern.

3 Caryatids
Sculptures of women used as columns. The most famous are at the Erechtheion at the Acropolis.

4 Pediment
The triangular gable supported by columns on the temple's façade; often features relief sculptures.

5 Frieze
The horizontal band running below the pediment of a temple, and carved with decorative motifs.

6 Krater
A large ceramic or bronze bowl, often beautifully decorated, used for mixing wine and water.

7 Black-Figure Pottery
The earliest type of Greek vase-painting, etched into red ceramic glaze, creating a somewhat stiff, formal image.

8 Red-Figure Pottery
A revolutionary method of Classical vase-painting. The outlines of figures are painted on with red glaze, creating flowing, active images.

9 Fresco
A painting made directly into the plaster before it has dried, creating art on the walls themselves.

10 Icon
Byzantine and Christian images of saints, believed to have holy power. They are often painted with gold.

Caryatids at the Erechtheion

🔟 Archaeological Sites

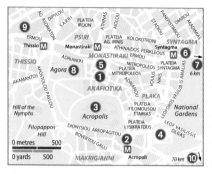

1 Roman Forum and Tower of the Winds

One of the city's most interestingly layered sites. Buildings and remains include the ingenious Tower of the Winds from 50 BC, the 1st-century AD Roman forum, and a mosque built by the Ottomans *(see pp24–5)*.

The Roman Forum

2 Acropolis Museum

The museum has been built over a late-Roman and early Byzantine settlement. The site is packed with houses and at least one fountain and reservoir, rare in the parched city. A walkway through the site and glass floors in the museum allow visitors to see all angles of it, a fascinating juxta-position to the earlier archaeological finds within the museum *(see pp14–15 and p77)*.

3 Acropolis

If you're only in Athens for a day, this is the one sight to see. The temples, especially the great Parthenon, built to honour Athena, have been the dominating influence in Western architecture for over 2,000 years. They continue to astonish and inspire *(see pp12–13 and p77)*.

4 Temple of Olympian Zeus

The colossal temple to Zeus was commissioned in 515 BC and took nearly 700 years to complete, during which time many other buildings – temples, baths and a law court – sprang up around it *(see pp36–7)*.

5 Hadrian's Library

Hadrian built this luxurious Corinthian-columned building in AD 132. Most of the space was a showy marble courtyard, with gardens and a pool. There were also lecture rooms, music rooms and a theatre. The library itself was on the east side, where you can see marble slots for manuscript scrolls *(see p84)*.

6 Syntagma Metro Station

In the late 1990s, Athens undertook its biggest archaeological dig ever: excavating a long-delayed metro – essential for hosting the Olympics. Many feared that the tightly scheduled dig would endanger what lay beneath. The Syntagma metro station was a brilliant compromise: though modern and gleaming, one glass wall looks directly through to an archaeological site, with detailed explanations of its various layers *(see p101)*.

Kesariani monastery

7 Kesariani
MAP T2 ■ 210 723 6619
■ 8am–3pm Tue–Sun ■ Adm

This 11th-century monastery on the cypress-clad slopes of Mount Hymettos makes a wonderful day trip (best reached by car). The chapel, dedicated to the Presentation of the Virgin, is built atop Classical ruins, and its walls are decorated with cloisonné (enamelled) masonry and late 17th-century paintings. The ram's-head fountain is said to cure infertility *(see p56)*.

8 Agora
The Agora, the marketplace where philosophers held forth, tradesmen bickered and statesmen hammered out the terms of the first democracy, was the city's heart and soul for 1200 years. This is one of the most hands-on sites in Athens and includes the Temple of Hephaestus, the best-preserved ancient Greek temple *(see pp16–17)*.

9 Kerameikos
This fascinating site around ancient Athens' walls should not be missed. It contains evidence of all the activities that take place at a city's edge: tombs (raised circular mounds for war heroes, pompous marble statues for great statesmen), temples, important roads, pottery workshops and a brothel. It's also a shady oasis in the congested city centre *(see pp30–31)*.

10 Temple of Poseidon
MAP T3 ■ 70 km (43 miles)
south of Athens on the Sounio Road
■ 229 203 9363 ■ 9:30am–sunset
daily ■ Adm

The great marble shrine to the sea god, situated on Cape Sounio's peak and surrounded by the Aegean Sea, is among the most stunning sights in all of Greece. It was built in the 5th century BC. British poet Lord Byron was one of many who fell under its spell 2,400 years later, composing poetry in its honour and carving his name on a pillar. Come at sunset, just before it closes, for a spectacular and unforgettable view.

Temple of Poseidon at Cape Sounio

🔟 Museums

and Asia, has filtered through the unique Hellenic sensibility. The array of beautiful instruments includes carved Byzantine lyres, ivory lutes and gypsy flutes *(see p78)*.

3 Acropolis Museum

This beautiful museum was designed partly to provide a fitting home to the famed marble sculptures of the Acropolis, and partly as a political gambit to force Britain to return the Parthenon marbles, which currently reside in the British Museum *(see pp14–15)*.

1 Agora Museum

The fascinating displays of finds from the city's ancient marketplace focus on objects used in the workings of the first democracy, including the declaration inscribed on marble that a government of democracy, not tyranny, was to rule *(see pp18–19)*.

2 Museum of Greek Musical Instruments

Greek musical instruments are far more varied than the bouzouki that plucked out the theme to *Zorba the Greek*. The Greek musical tradition, though heavily influenced by Turkey

4 National Gallery of Art

■ Army Park in Goudi, Panagiotis Kanellopoulos Ave ■ 9am– 6pm Mon–Thu. Closed Sun ■ Adm

Greece's most important art gallery, showing the greatest works of Greek artists. Masterpieces by El Greco (known in his homeland by his real name, Domenikos Theotokopoulos) are the highlight of the collection. This location is a temporary space for the gallery while the original site is undergoing reconstruction.

Display of bouzouki and lutes at the Museum of Greek Musical Instruments

5 Benaki Museum

Follow the progress of Greek art and culture through this first-rate collection from the eras of antiquity to the mid-20th century. Walk through excellently presented displays in the gorgeous Neo-Classical mansion of the Benaki family *(see pp26–7)*.

6 National Archaeological Museum

One of the world's most important museums, featuring a jaw-dropping array of treasures from the ancient and Classical Greek civilizations. Don't miss the exquisite frescoes of 17th-century-BC Thira, and the golden hoard of splendid prehistoric Mycenae *(see pp20–21)*.

Liturgical object at the Museum of Greek Folk Art

embroideries, costumes, shadow puppets and filigreed jewellery, from the mainland and the Aegean Islands. The collection also covers the renaissance of decorative crafts in the 18th and 19th centuries. The museum is currently closed and will reopen in a new location in 2018 *(see p78)*.

9 War Museum

A lengthy display of warfare in Greece, beginning with prehistoric battle-axes, running through Alexander the Great's battle plans and the Greek War of Independence to the present. The Saroglos collection includes medieval swords, Renaissance foils and duelling pistols, engraved Turkish scimitars and samurai blades. Unfortunately, the accompanying information is scarce and only in Greek *(see p103)*.

10 Byzantine and Christian Museum

Yet another of the top museums in the world. There are over 15,000 objects from the greatest Byzantine churches and monasteries worldwide, including sculpture, manuscripts, icons, frescoes and precious, eye-strainingly intricate gold, silver and gem-encrusted ecclesiastical objects *(see pp32–3)*.

National Archaeological Museum

7 Museum of Cycladic Art

The Cycladic island civilization of the Aegean flourished at the same time as the early Egyptians and Mesopotamians, but produced something very different: strangely elegant, stylized marble goddess-cult figurines. These were the first pieces in the centuries-long tradition of Greek art that was to follow and this is the world's largest collection *(see pp22–3 and p102)*.

8 Museum of Greek Folk Art

A rich collection of Greek folk art from 1650 to the present day, including traditional tapestries,

Byzantine and Christian Museum

🔟 Churches

1 Church of the Metamorphosis (Sotiros)

MAP C5 ■ Theorias St, Upper Plaka

This Byzantine church is situated on the northern slope of the Acropolis and dates back either to the second half of the 11th century or the 14th century. It is a four-columned church with a tall Athenian dome, typical of monuments from this period. The dome and the northern and southern sides have remained intact, but the western sides have been rebuilt.

2 Monastiraki

Once the greatest monastery of the area, this is the church from which the Monastiraki neighbourhood takes its name. "Little monastery" was so called after the destruction of its many surrounding buildings during 19th-century archaeological digs. It has since been restored (see p86).

3 Kesariani, Mount Hymettos

This 12th-century monastery sits on fragrant, wooded slopes just outside Athens. Most of its surviving frescoes are from the 16th and 17th centuries, and its rushing spring waters are said to cure infertility (see p53).

4 Agii Apostoli
MAP J4

The Church of the Holy Apostles is one of Athens' oldest churches, built in the early 11th century over a 2nd-century monument in the ancient Agora. Though it underwent a great deal of damage during the Ottoman occupation, the remains of its frescoes have been preserved and restored within.

Agii Apostoli

Interior of Kapnikarea

5 Kapnikarea

This lovely little church, dedicated to the Virgin Mary, was built in the 11th century over the ruins of an ancient temple. It is laid out in the typical Byzantine cross-in-square plan, with three apses on the east side and a narthex (a western portico) on the west. Inside, the church is decorated with medieval mosaics (see p87).

6 Panagia Grigoroussa
MAP J4 ■ By Tower of the Winds ■ Services Apr–Oct: 5:45pm; Nov–Mar: 4:45pm

If you've lost something, this is the place to go. Every Saturday, this famous church holds services blessing tasty *fanouropita* cakes. Once eaten, they are supposed to help you find what you're looking for.

7 Agios Georgios
MAP P1

Claiming the highest point in modern-day Athens – the peak of Lykavittos Hill – Agios Georgios boasts views as far as the Saronic Gulf, the island of Aegina and the Peloponnese coast. Services are held both inside and outside.

8 Panagia Gorgoepikoos

Dwarfed by the bulk of Mitropoli, tiny Panagia Gorgoepikoos (Mikri Mitropoli, "little Mitropoli") actually far outshadows its vast neighbour in historic and artistic importance. It was built in the 12th century, on the ruins of an ancient temple dedicated to goddess Eileithyia. Its walls are built entirely of Roman and Byzantine marble relics, sculpted with reliefs depicting the ancient calendar of feasts (see also Mitropoli entry on p79).

9 Agia Ekaterini

Fragments of Classical columns remain in the courtyard of this beautiful 12th-century church – it too was built over the ruins of an ancient temple, this one possibly dedicated to the goddess Hestia. The church's many colourful frescoes have been lovingly restored (see p80).

Religious art in Mitropoli

10 Mitropoli

Athens' massive cathedral of 1862 was the first major church built after Greece's independence. It became the seat of the archbishop and hence of modern Greek orthodoxy. Though its colourful frescoes and pricey ecclesiastical objects are certainly impressive, its architecture is less so. Mitropoli's importance is almost entirely spiritual, as the focal point for the Greek Orthodox Church (see also p79).

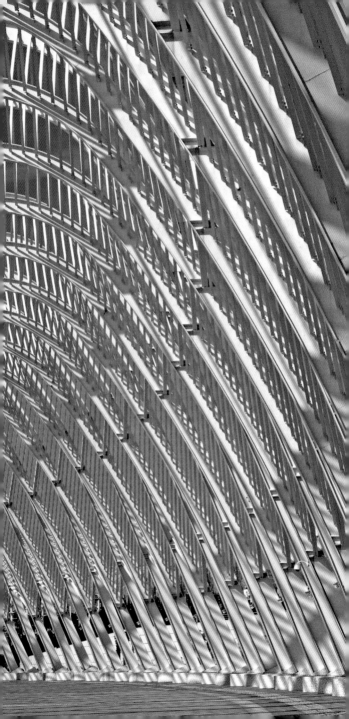

City Strolls

Ermou, Athens' main shopping street

Ermou

The shopping street. Start at the top, with designer boutiques and department stores, then make your way down to the funkier end, most obviously when Sunday's flea market *(see p87)* fills the street. Beyond it are loads of quirky used-furniture, antiques and speciality shops.

2 Dionysiou Areopagitou Walkway

This wide, tree-lined walkway provides a continuous pedestrian link between all the major archaeological sites in central Athens, and has several open-air cafés.

3 Kallidromiou and Strefi Hill

Kallidromiou is the heart of Exarcheia, especially on Saturdays, when the whole neighbourhood turns out for the open-air *laiki* (farmer's market). Soak up the sights of the street and buy some fresh fruit before heading to nearby Strefi Hill *(see p95)* for a healthy climb and bite to eat.

4 Filopappos Hill

Follow the winding paths to different monuments including two Byzantine churches, a Roman memorial and Athens' old observatory. At the summit of this shady hill, enjoy extensive views over and beyond the city *(see pp34–5)*.

5 First National Cemetery of Athens

MAP D–E6

Take a contemplative walk through the wide, overgrown rows of handsome mausoleums in Athens' largest cemetery. It is thickly planted with cypress trees, whose tall, pointed shape the Greeks believe helps to guide souls up to heaven.

6 Lykavittos Hill

Several pleasant footpaths run through pine-clad Lykavittos Hill. If you're feeling energetic, hike to the top; if climbing's not for you, take the funicular up and saunter down, stopping at the café for a drink *(see p102)*.

Walking up Lykavittos Hill, overlooking the city

7 Pasalimani
This natural harbour at Piraeus is full of local fishing boats and yachts. Stroll around the marina, ending up on the east side, in front of the Nautical Museum, or come after dark when the many waterside cafés come to life (see p111).

8 Kallimarmaro Stadium
Fourth-century BC Panathenaic athletes and the runners of the first modern Olympics in 1896 ran laps in the sweltering centre of this beautiful marble stadium. Modern joggers and walkers love the shady path on top of the 70,000-seat edifice (see p101).

National Gardens

9 National Gardens
The winding paths of the lush National Gardens are a great place to stroll. In 1839, when this was a royal park, the landscape was densely planted with 15,000 exotic trees and flowers imported from around the world; many of those original plants still flourish (see p101).

10 Flisvos Marina
For a taste of cosmopolitan Athens, head to Flisvos Marina, where some of the most impressive yachts in the Mediterranean dock. A stroll along the promenade takes you past an outdoor shopping centre plus restaurants and cafés with sea views.

TOP 10 CITY VIEWS

Views from Areopagus rock

1 Areopagus
This high, slippery rock jutting over the Agora is where, for centuries, Athens' ruling council met.

2 Orizontes Restaurant
Watch the glittering nighttime cityscape from Orizontes on Lykavittos Hill (see p107).

3 Filopappos Monument
Spectacular views directly across to the temples of the Acropolis or to Piraeus and the coast. (See p34.)

4 Adrianou, Monastiraki
Sit in one of the many outdoor cafés lining this street for a ring-side view of the ancient marketplace (see p88).

5 Athens 360
A classic Monastiraki rooftop bar and café with prime views of the Acropolis.

6 Galaxy Bar
A popular spot for the fashionable set, the bar on the top floor of the Hilton Hotel offers stunning views over Athens (see p144).

7 Strefi Hill
In the shadow of Lykavittos, this green hill (see p95) is perfect if you desire a shorter climb but comparable views.

8 Athens Tower Mesogeion 2
Greece's tallest building; no observation deck, but great views if you're visiting any of its companies.

9 Kesariani Monastery
Lovely monastery on the wooded slopes of Mount Hymettos, above Athens' northern suburbs (see p53).

10 Mount Penteli
Up by the National Observatory in Athens' northernmost suburb, you get a great view of the city – day or night.

🔟 Off the Beaten Track

① The Breeder Gallery

MAP B2 ■ Iasonos 45, Metaxourgio ■ noon–6pm Tue–Sat ■ www. thebreedersystem.com

West of Omonia, the up-and-coming (if somewhat seedy) neighbourhood of Metaxourgio is home to a growing number of art galleries, museums and trendy restaurants and cafés. The oldest and best-known gallery, The Breeder, showcases contemporary art, promoting emerging Greek talent as well as exhibiting works by established international artists.

② Athens Food Walk

MAP C4 ■ Meet at Plateia Monastiraki ■ 10am Mon–Sat ■ Reservations essential ■ www.alternativeathens.com

Revealing local shopping haunts, this three-hour tour, run by Alternative Athens, takes you to family-run food stores and delicatessens around Monastiraki and Psiri, as well as the Central Market. Arrive hungry – there's lots of tasting along the way.

A stop on the Athens Food Walk

③ Grigoropoulos Shrine

MAP D2 ■ Tzavella, Exarcheia

Commemorating 15-year-old Alexandros Grigoropoulos, who was killed by the police in 2008, this small shrine lies on a pedestrianized alley in bohemian Exarcheia. Marked by a marble plaque, flickering candles and flowers, it is a gathering point for left-wing students and anarchists.

④ Street Art Tour

MAP C2 ■ Meet at Plateia Omonia ■ 6pm Wed ■ Reservations essential ■ www.atathens.org

Athens is known for its graffiti artists, who make political statements with colour and humour on walls around the city. This three-hour tour, run by Alternative Tours of Athens, takes you through the edgy neighbourhoods of Exarcheia and Metaxourgio, to reveal some of the city's most impressive graffiti.

⑤ Sarri 12 Gallery

MAP B3 ■ Sarri 12, Psiri ■ noon–5pm Wed–Sun ■ www.sarri12.com

In Psiri, this tiny gallery showcases some of Europe's most innovative street artists. Founded in 2013, it has hosted exhibitions by locals such as Sonke, Opium and Cacao

Rocks, as well as celebrated London-based artists Malarko Hernandez and David Shillinglaw.

6 Cine Thision

MAP B5 ■ Apostolou Pavlou 7, Thissio ■ May–Sep, screenings 9pm & 11pm ■ Adm ■ cine-thisio.gr

Hidden behind a wall, opposite the Agora, Athens' oldest *therino* (open-air cinema) dates from 1935. Locals flock here for outdoor films on balmy summer evenings. There's a bar for drinks and a magical view of the floodlit Acropolis. Films are in their original version, with Greek subtitles.

7 Greek Wine's Rebirth Uncorked

MAP K3 ■ Meet on Plateia Mitropoleos, Plaka ■ 5pm Sat ■ Reservations essential ■ www.culinarybackstreets.com

This three-hour wine-tasting tour, run by Athens Culinary Backstreets, takes you to several small local wine bars, to taste ten different wines from Crete, Santorini, Naoussa and Nemea. It's led by a sommelier, who will talk about the history of Greek winemaking.

8 Glyfada Beach

MAP T3 ■ Glyfada, 16 km (10 miles) from Athens, Attica coast ■ May–Oct ■ Adm

Few European capitals have beaches so close to the city centre. The tram from Syntagma takes you directly to Glyfada, a residential suburb with a sandy beach. In summer, locals arrive during their lunch break, take a dip, then go back to work. Stunning sunsets too.

Glyfada Beach

9 Kesariani Monastery

MAP T2 ■ Kesariani ■ 210 723 6619 ■ 8am–3:30pm Tue–Sun ■ Adm

A 25-minute bus ride from Syntagma, followed by a short walk up the lower slopes of Mount Hymettus, brings you to this 11th-century Orthodox monastery, set amid unspoilt nature. There's a Byzantine church with lovely frescoes, plus the ruins of the refectory, monks' cells and a bathhouse. It is occasionally visited by tour groups but, if you're lucky, it will be deserted.

Kesariani Monastery

10 Spa at the Divani Apollon Palace & Thalasso

MAP T3 ■ Agiou Nikolaou 10, Vouliagmeni ■ 210 891 1100 ■ 10am–10pm Mon–Fri, 10am–8pm Sat, 11am–7pm Sun ■ www.divani apollonhotel.com/spa.html

For relaxation and revitalization, visit Athens' largest spa, on the coast at Vouliagmeni. Centred on an indoor seawater pool with underwater jets, it offers beauty treatments, a range of massages, hammam, sauna and an ultra-modern gym.

🔟 Restaurants

1 Cookoovaya

This experimental restaurant brings together five noted Greek chefs in a modern, open-plan kitchen. Try the beef carpaccio with gorgonzola, or the octopus with fava bean purée *(see p107)*.

Elegant dining at Cookoovaya

2 Mana's Kouzina-Kouzina

MAP K3 ■ Aiolou 27 ■ 210 325 2335 ■ €€

Set in a historic square with views of the Acropolis, Mana's Kouzina-Kouzina ("mother's kitchen") specializes in regional Greek dishes. The menu is based on local produce.

3 Funky Gourmet, Gazi-Metaxourgio

Serving three degustation menus (no à la carte), the Michelin-starred Funky Gourmet specializes in molecular gastronomy based on Mediterranean ingredients. Dinner here is a real event in itself – theatrical, sensual and full of surprises *(see p90)*.

4 Varoulko Seaside, Mikrolimano, Piraeus

Celebrity chef Lefteris Lazarou serves creative seafood dishes at waterside tables overlooking Mikrolimano. Dishes such as grilled squid with black-eyed beans, marjoram and cumin, and oven-baked John Dory with cauliflower purée have earned him a Michelin star *(see p114)*.

5 Mani Mani

Greek-American brothers add international style and a delicate, inspired touch to the cuisine here. Menu highlights include pork tenderloin with goat's cheese, figs, honey and almonds, or the vegetable tower *(see p83)*.

6 Milos

Costas Spiliades, founder of New York's highly acclaimed Estiatorio Milos, has opened a sister restaurant in Athens' Hilton Hotel. Expect exquisite Greek seafood dishes, a luxurious setting and impeccable service *(see p107)*.

7 Aleria, Gazi-Metaxourgio

A fine choice for a romantic dinner for two, Aleria serves tasty contemporary cuisine, with favourites such as pumpkin mousse with truffles, and couscous *bourdeto* (Corfiot fish stew) with scorpion fish, mussels and squid. To try several dishes, opt for the reasonably priced five-course degustation menu *(see p90)*.

Romantic setting at Aleria

Two Michelin-starred Spondi

⑧ Spondi

The most sophisticated restaurant in Greece boasts two Michelin stars and offers exquisitely prepared and presented haute cuisine by French chef Arnaud Bignon. Try dishes such as crab in herb jelly or venison in Sarawak pepper crust *(see p107)*.

Hytra, Onassis Cultural Centre

⑨ Hytra

MAP T2 ▪ Onassis Cultural Centre, Syngrou 107–9
▪ 210 331 6767 ▪ €€€

Michelin-starred chef Tasos Mantis serves a modern take on traditional Greek dishes, including quail, milk-fed goat and sea bass. There is also a vegetarian degustation menu.

⑩ Orizontes

Perched on Lykavittos Hill, Orizontes is an unforgettable dining venue. The city views are stunning, and the creative Mediterranean cuisine and extensive wine list are both excellent *(see p107)*.

TOP 10 TAVERNAS

1 Klimataria
MAP J1 ▪ Plateia Theatrou 2
▪ 210 321 6629 ▪ €
A lively, historic taverna popular with locals due to its rembetika music, dancing and excellent dishes.

2 Tzitsikas & Mermingas
Traditional Greek dishes with modern twists are on the menu at this cheerful and popular taverna *(see p107)*.

3 Filipou
MAP F3 ▪ Xenokratous 19
▪ 210 721 6390 ▪ €
Old-world taverna in Athens' poshest neighbourhood.

4 Bakaliarakia tou Damigou
An underground hideaway with justly famous fried cod and its very own ancient column *(see p83)*.

5 Yiantes
Enjoy a variety of Greek dishes prepared with mainly organic ingredients in a pretty walled courtyard *(see p98)*.

6 To Kafenion
Delicious traditional food is served in cosy surroundings *(see p83)*.

7 Tou Psarra
One of the few unspoiled garden tavernas in Plaka *(see p83)*.

8 Sholarhio
A traditional family taverna in the centre of Plaka with a menu of typical Greek specialities *(see p83)*.

9 O Platanos
The place to go to for the authentic Greek-taverna experience *(see p83)*.

10 Rififi
A contemporary taverna with a summery pink-and-sea-green decor. Try the delicious filo-wrapped feta with honey *(see p98)*.

Relaxed and fun Rififi

For a key to restaurant price ranges see p83

TOP 10 Greek Dishes

1 Moussaka
There are endless variations on this famous country casserole, but the basic ingredients – aubergine (eggplant) and minced lamb layered with potatoes and tomatoes, enriched with wine, spiced with cinnamon and topped with bechamel – stay the same. The flavour is warming and earthy.

2 Stifado
This rich, tender wild rabbit stew comes from the mountains of northern Greece, where it still warms villagers every winter. The rabbit is spiced with cumin, cloves and cinnamon, but its most wonderful characteristic is an unusual sweetness, achieved by the addition of lots of small onions, cooked until caramelized.

3 Horiatiki
A bastardized version appears on menus worldwide as "Greek salad". The real thing is just a matter of fresh ingredients. Sun-ripened tomatoes, crisp cucumbers, crunchy red onions and green peppers, rich Kalamata olives, topped with a slab of feta, aromatic oregano and extra-virgin olive oil make up this simple but halcyon salad.

Grilled octopus

Stifado, or **rabbit stew**

4 Grilled Octopus
Best caught and served on the same day, having been grilled over hot coals, topped with a squeeze of lemon and drizzled with oil and vinegar. The texture should be tender and the taste salty-sweet.

5 Pittes
Pittes came to Greece from Turkey and the Middle East. The key to perfect *pittes* (which means "pies") is the famous filo crust: dozens of layers of paper-thin, translucent dough, brushed with butter or olive oil and baked to light, flaky perfection. Fillings range from sweet (the honey, walnut and rosewater baklava) to savoury – spinach and feta or *hortopita*, made from wild greens.

6 Kokoretsi
New EU food laws have made this essential Easter dish technically illegal, but in back gardens and old-time tavernas Greeks continue to serve it year round. They take the intestines of lamb, marinate them in herbs, garlic and lemon juice, and roast the whole thing for hours over coals, until it drips with flavourful juices.

Horiatiki

7 Gemista

The name simply means "stuffed". Greeks pack tomatoes, aubergines, courgettes (zucchini), peppers and vine leaves with all manner of ingredients, including rice, herbs, mince, raisins, pine nuts and an array of spices. Often topped with a creamy, lemony sauce, *gemista* make a fulfilling meal on their own.

8 Fassolada

The staple winter dish for the ancient Greeks, *fassolada* is still Greece's most popular soup. White beans, carrots, onions, tomatoes and oregano are simmered in stock until tender, then topped with the crucial ingredient: extra-virgin olive oil. In summer, cold *fassolada* is often served as a meze in the afternoon.

Souvlaki on a bed of vegetables

9 Souvlaki

Souvla means spit-roasted, and this is the Greeks' favourite way to serve meat. *Souvlaki* refers to the ubiquitous street favourite: hunks of chicken, pork or lamb spit-roasted for hours. They are often lathered with tzatziki, and stuffed along with onions and tomatoes into a hot, freshly baked, oiled and fried bread-dough.

10 Kokkinisto

This is a simple, classic taverna dish, whose name means "red-sauced". Lamb, chicken or pork is cooked with tomatoes, wine and herbs in a clay pot, which keeps in all the moisture and pungent flavour. The tender, infused meat should fall off the bone at the mere touch of a fork.

TOP 10 GREEK DRINKS

Ouzo

1 Ouzo
Greece wouldn't be the same without this spirit. Drunk with mezes, this aniseed-flavoured distillate packs a powerful punch.

2 Tsipouro
Made from the residue left after distilling Muscatel grapes, fiery, warming *tsipouro* does its job best in winter months.

3 Retsina
The taste is not subtle, but the affection for this wine with pine resin cuts across all age and class barriers.

4 Hima
Home-made barrel wine, often poured into pitchers or plastic bottles directly from casks on the taverna wall.

5 Mavrodaphne
The name translates as "black laurel". The best grapes for this rich, dark, port-like sweet wine come from the Peloponnese.

6 Aghiorghitiko
Deep, velvety "St George" wines from Nemea are the rising stars of the growing Greek wine industry.

7 Assyrtiko
Greece's finest white wine – one of the most unusual in the Mediterranean – is redolent of honeysuckle and figs.

8 Savatiano
Greece's most common white wine is great with seafood and salads. It is most often found in tavernas.

9 Greek Coffee
Thick, sweet, pungent mud of strong, black coffee. Ask for an *elliniko metrio*.

10 Frappé
Nescafé, milk and cold water whipped into a pleasant, cool froth.

Places to Shop

① Folli Follie

Now a major player with more than 600 points of sale worldwide, Folli Follie was established in Greece in 1982. Fashion-conscious women flock to this store in search of accessories such as jewellery, watches, bags and belts. The philosophy behind the brand is affordable luxury *(see p105)*.

② Loumidis Coffee Shop

The oldest remaining coffee roaster in Greece. This caffeine-fancier's paradise stocks a wealth of traditional Greek coffees, plus all the paraphernalia necessary for its preparation. It also sells a range of beans from around the world, as well as espresso machines, cups, shakers and all the accoutrements one could possibly desire for that perfect cup of coffee *(see p97)*.

③ Melissinos Art

Come here for made-to-measure handcrafted leather sandals, inspired by ancient Greek designs – the perfect footwear for a summer on the beach. Melissinos' famous customers have included The Beatles, Leonard Cohen and Kate Moss *(see p89)*.

Baklava from Karavan

④ Karavan

MAP M2 ■ Voukourestiou 11
■ 210 364 1540

A tiny treasure trove of sweet treats, Karavan sells the best baklava and *kataifi* (pastries made with shredded dough) in town.

Athens' Flea Market

⑤ Athens' Flea Market

If you have an eye for an authentic antique, you can pick up outstanding bargains at this sprawling and varied Sunday market. Wake up early, though – there's not much point arriving here after 11am, as the streets become jam-packed and most of the treasures disappear quickly *(see p87)*.

⑥ Elena Votsi

Elena Votsi's items are available in London, Paris and New York, but the full range can be viewed at her boutique in Athens. Votsi works mainly with gold, lapis lazuli, coral, amethyst and aquamarine, and her trademarks are thick-set, rough-cut necklaces and knuckle-duster rings. Votsi is also known as the designer of the front of the Olympic summer games medal *(see p105)*.

7 Korres
MAP D4 ▪ Ermou 4, Syntagma

The humble origins of this natural-based, environmentally and animal-friendly cosmetics brand that has taken Europe and the United States by storm lie in this small homeopathic pharmacy. The full collection of haircare, suncare, and face and body lotions is available here. Delight the senses with refreshing citrus body spray, the sweetly spicy coriander shower gel or the orange blossom facial cleanser.

8 Zoumboulakis Gallery
MAP M3 ▪ Kriezotou 6
▪ 210 364 0264

A veritable Athenian institution, this shop showcases contemporary art, furniture, ceramics and sculptures. Also, there is an excellent range of limited-edition prints and posters by established artists, and exhibitions are held by up-and-coming Greek artists. Signed and numbered silkscreens are reasonably priced.

9 Kori

Bringing a new quality and sophistication to the words souvenir shop, Kori stocks an eclectic mix of accessories and ornaments crafted by some of Greece's brightest and best young artists, as well as replicas of museum pieces and traditional pottery, icons and statuettes (see p81).

10 Pantopolion

A treasure trove for gourmets, this store stocks an assortment of quality Greek regional produce, including thyme honey from Tinos, Mastiha liqueur from Chios, black olives from Kalamata, and dried herbs and teas from Mount Taygetos. Pantopolion is run by two retired lawyers, who also offer talks and organize tastings, and will gladly package a selection of items in presentation boxes for you to take home (see p89).

Kori, a treasure trove of elegant Greek souvenirs

🔟 Athens for Free

A busker on Plateia Monastiraki

1 Street Performers
Pass by Plateia Monastiraki (see p86) at almost any time of day to be entertained by street artists, who perform everything from mime acts and fire-eating, to juggling and busking.

2 Acropolis for Free
There is free entry to the Acropolis (see pp12–13) on 6 Mar (in memory of Melina Mercouri), 18 Apr (International Monuments Day), 18 May (International Museums Day), 5 Jun (International Environment Day), the last weekend of Sep (European Heritage Day), 18 Oct (Ohi Day) and every first Sun of the month from 1 Nov to 31 Mar. The same applies to the National Archaeological Museum (see pp20–21).

3 Benaki Museum for Free
The Benaki Museum (see pp26–7) in Kolonaki traces the development of Greek culture through the ages and offers free entry every Thursday, when it also has extended opening hours, 9am–midnight.

4 Byzantine Break
On the busy shopping street of Ermou, take a look inside tiny Kapnikarea (see p87), a peaceful Byzantine church animated by flickering candles and bearded priests amid wafts of incense.

5 European Music Day
Each year on 21 June (the longest day of the year), free, open-air concerts take place throughout Greece, with the main stage in Athens on Plateia Kotzia near Plateia Omonia (see p93). Past performers include Transglobal Underground and Scissor Sisters.

6 Seaside Stroll
From Neo Faliro metro station, you can walk all the way along the coast to Piraeus, passing the fishing boats in the harbour at Microlimano (see p113), flashy yachts moored up in Pasalimani (see p111) and informal cafés with fine sea views along Akti Themistokleous (see p112).

Moored fishing boats and yachts in Piraeus

7 Musical Enlightenment

You can discover more about the sound, appearance and history of traditional Greek musical instruments at the educational and amusing Museum of Greek Musical Instruments *(see p54 and p78)* in Plaka, which offers free entry throughout the year.

8 Performing Soldiers

Every Sunday at 11am, you can watch the *evzones* (soldiers) at the ceremonial Changing of the Guard next to the Tomb of the Unknown Soldier, in front of the Parliament *(see p101)*, on Plateia Syntagma.

Changing of the Guard ceremony

9 Panoramic Views

For a total escape from the urban bustle, hike up a steep winding path to the top of Lykavittos Hill *(see p102)* to enjoy glorious panoramic views over the entire city, with the sea and mountains visible in the distance. Great photo opportunities – and a free workout, too.

10 Market Colours

The Central Market *(see p94)* offers an authentic Athenian shopping experience. You don't have to buy anything, but the stalls – piled high with seasonal fruit and vegetables, fresh seafood displayed on crushed ice and slightly gory meat products – make this a great venue for capturing local colour and atmosphere.

TOP 10 MONEY-SAVING TIPS

Travelling by ferry

1 Tap water in Athens is perfectly good to drink, so you don't have to buy bottled mineral water.

2 When eating out, opt for barrel wine, which will be served by the carafe. It's cheap and cheerful, while bottled wine tends to be expensive.

3 Most the main attractions in central Athens are within walking distance of one another, so you rarely need to use public transport. Just be sure to wear comfortable shoes.

4 If you use public transport, be aware that a one-day travel ticket (valid for bus, tram and metro) costs €4.50; a five-day ticket €9. Senior EU citizens with ID cards receive a 50 per cent discount.

5 Greek *souvlaki* makes a tasty and nutritious takeaway meal, and is a cheap alternative to a sit-down lunch.

6 Online private rental sites such as Airbnb offer comfortable and often central accommodation in privately owned apartments, which are generally cheaper than hotels.

7 If you're making a trip to the nearby islands, remember that ferries are much cheaper (although slower) than hydrofoils and catamarans.

8 The Acropolis entrance ticket (valid three days) gives you access to 10 other ancient sites, so be sure to keep it safe to avoid paying twice.

9 The National Archaeological Museum ticket package gives you access to the Byzantine and Christian Museum, the Numismatic Museum and the Epigraphical Museum.

10 At the beach, you have to pay for a sun bed, so take a towel and lie on the sand to avoid the extra cost.

Festivals and Events

1 Epiphany (6 Jan)
The "Blessing of the Waters", when ports, boats and beaches are blessed, and young men dive for crosses cast into the water by priests; it's a year's good luck for the successful divers.

2 Apokries (Feb–Mar)
The Greek Orthodox Carnival begins 58 days before Easter. Festivities, especially glamorous masquerade parties, last for days. In Athens, the colourful celebrations centre on Plaka, where the streets are packed with celebrants and masked musicians.

Flying kites on Clean Monday

3 Clean Monday
Greeks celebrate the first day of Lent by going to the country and flying kites; in Athens, the sky above Filopappos Hill is usually filled with them.

4 Independence Day (25 Mar)
Full-on military parades with tanks, guns and battalions celebrate the date in 1821 when, after nearly 400 years of occupation, the Greek revolution successfully rose up against the Ottoman Empire.

Eggs dyed red for Easter

5 Easter
This is the most important event on the Orthodox calendar, far outweighing Christmas. On the night of Easter Friday, participants follow effigies of Jesus on flower-covered biers in candlelit processions, concluding in midnight services and fireworks (and, in mountain villages, rounds of gunshots). On Sunday, families gather to enjoy a meal of roast lamb, and also eat eggs dyed red (symbolizing both the blood and rebirth of Christ).

6 Athens and Epidauros Festival (Jun–Sep)
www.greekfestival.gr
Ancient Greeks performed their timeless tragedies in the spectacular Odeon of Herodes Atticus and the theatre of Epidauros. Now, every summer, the world's greatest singers, dancers and actors perform under moonlight in these venues. Recent singers include the Harlem Gospel Choir, while Gérard Depardieu and Isabella Rossellini have performed in classical works at Epidauros.

Independence Day military parade

7 Rockwave (Jul)

www.rockwavefestival.gr

This three-day festival is Greece's hottest music ticket of the year. The line-up includes huge Greek and international pop, rock and alternative acts.

8 Feast of the Virgin (15 Aug)

Absolutely everything in town closes for the Assumption of the Virgin, which is second only to Easter in the Orthodox calendar. The full cross-section of Greek womanhood packs churches, as every "Maria" turns out to honour her namesake.

9 Ohi Day (28 Oct)

A national holiday, Ohi Day celebrates Greece's decisive "no" to Mussolini during World War II. A big military parade, culminating at Plateia Syntagma, is staged in Athens.

Athens Marathon

10 Athens Marathon (early Nov)

Athletes from around the world retrace the course of Pheidippidis, antiquity's most celebrated runner. In 490 BC, the Greeks defeated the Persians at Marathon in a historic battle for democracy (see p130). Pheidippidis ran the 42 km (26 miles) to Athens, announced the outcome ("Victory!"), then died of exhaustion. Today's runners have the advantage of water stops and cheering crowds en route from Marathonas to the Kallimarmaro Stadium (see p101) to ease the arduous feat.

TOP 10 SAINTS' DAYS

St Nicholas Day celebrations

1 St Basil (1 Jan)
Families eat *Vasilopita* (Basil's cake), into which coins have been baked. Finding a coin brings a year's good luck.

2 St John the Baptist (7 Jan)
The day John baptized Christ in the Jordan river. Various regional traditions involve dunking local men in water.

3 St Athanassios (18 Jan)
Today the church auctions off donated gifts in honour of Athanassios, one of Orthodoxy's three holy Fathers.

4 St Charalambos (10 Feb)
An important day for Greek hospitals which today honour the patron saint of physicians.

5 St George (23 Apr)
The dragon-slayer is the patron saint of the military, who honour him today.

6 St Dimitrios (26 Oct)
The greatest celebrations are in Thessaloniki, where this martyr, whose wounds ran with myrrh instead of blood, is patron saint.

7 St Catherine (25 Nov)
This famous martyr is honoured as the protectress of infants, maidens and students.

8 St Stelianos (26 Nov)
Pregnant women stay at home from work to ask Stelianos, patron of infants and childbirth, to protect their children.

9 St Barbara (4 Dec)
Mothers sometimes make their children sleep in a church on the night of St Barbara to protect them from illness.

10 St Nicholas (6 Dec)
Celebrations in honour of the patron saint of sailors are especially festive on islands and in coastal areas.

Athens Area by Area

The 4th-century theatre at Delphi

TOP 10 Plaka, Makrigianni and Koukaki

The winding alleyways of Plaka, the old quarter below the Acropolis, are easily the most charming part of Athens. Naturally, they are also the most visited, and in midsummer some streets can be packed with touts and cheap gift stalls. But Plaka also conceals places of untouched delight. The working-class areas of Makrigianni and Koukaki are shaking off old dust, and must-see museums, fine-dining restaurants and ultra-hip clubs are the new order of the day.

Sculpture, Roman Forum and Tower of the Winds

AREA MAP OF PLAKA, MAKRIGIANNI AND KOUKAKI

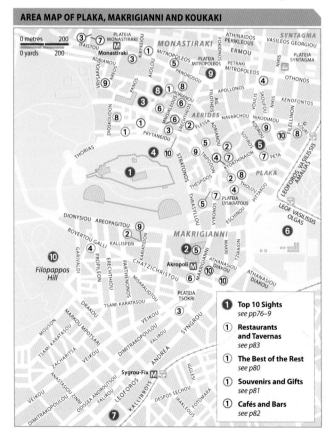

1	**Top 10 Sights**	see pp76–9
1	**Restaurants and Tavernas**	see p83
1	**The Best of the Rest**	see p80
1	**Souvenirs and Gifts**	see p81
1	**Cafés and Bars**	see p82

The impressive Acropolis, dominating the Plaka skyline

1 Acropolis

The sacred rock of the Acropolis dominates Plaka, and its different temples are clearly visible from all angles throughout the neighbourhood. Legend holds that it was on this rock that Athena (see p47) won dominion of Athens from Poseidon, and it has been devoted to worshipping the goddess since 650 BC (see also pp12–13 and p52).

2 Acropolis Museum

Designed by internationally renowned architect Bernard Tschumi, this all-glass $100 million museum opened in mid-2009. It was built with the intention to provide a fitting home to Greece's greatest treasures: the marble sculptures and architectural features that once adorned the Acropolis, especially the mighty Parthenon (see also pp14–15, p52 and p54).

Statue, Acropolis Museum

3 Roman Forum and Tower of the Winds

Julius Caesar and Augustus were founders of this Roman marketplace, which replaced the original Greek Agora, and their names are inscribed on the Gate of Athena Archegetis. But its most striking feature, the Tower of the Winds, was built in 50 BC, 100 years earlier. There was no other building like it in the ancient world: eight-sided, each side sculpted with a personification of the winds: Boreas, Kaikias, Apeliotes, Euros, Notos, Lips, Zephyros and Skiron (see also pp24–5 and p52).

4 Anafiotika

Clinging to the side of the Acropolis is Athens' loveliest and quirkiest neighbourhood. It was built in the 1800s by tradesmen from the Cycladic island of Anafi, brought to Athens after the War of Independence to build King Otto's palace. They re-created a pocket of home here, all island-style, blue-and-white houses, covered with banks of bougainvillea, in a maze of tiny passageways. Many descendants of the original Anafi workers still live here.

Peaceful courtyard in Anafiotika

LORD BYRON

Among Plaka's many famous residents was Romantic poet and philhellene Lord Byron (1788–1824), who lived in a monastery on Plateia Lysikratous while writing *Childe Harold*. He fought on the Greek side in the War of Independence, and Athens remembers him in a street off the square named after him: Vyronas, in Greek.

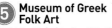

Museum of Greek Folk Art

5 Museum of Greek Folk Art

MAP L4 ▪ Kydathinaion 17 ▪ 210 322 9031 ▪ Limited info in English ▪ Adm ▪ www.melt.gr

This museum has a vast collection of rich, beautiful folk art, from jewellery to decorate and cover the entire body to fine embroideries worked with gold and silver thread. Also included are traditional tapestries and shadow puppets. The museum is closed until 2018, when it will reopen in a new location (see p55).

6 Temple of Olympian Zeus

 All that remains of Greece's largest temple, a shrine to Zeus, is 16 columns. But, as they stand alone, silhouetted by the bright Attic sky, their majesty still overwhelms. Inside the temple was a colossal gold-and-ivory sculpture of the god, a copy of the one at Olympus, which was one of the Seven Wonders of the ancient world (see also pp36–7).

7 National Museum of Contemporary Art

MAP C6 ▪ Kallirois & Frantzi, Makrigianni ▪ 210 924 2111/3 ▪ Adm ▪ www.emst.gr

The long-awaited National Museum of Contemporary Art (EMST) is due to open in 2017 in the Fix building, a former brewery dating from 1957. It will display works by both Greek and foreign artists, including photography by Nan Goldin; video installations by Bill Viola, Nam June Paik and Marina Abramović; sculpture by Stephen Antonakos; and paintings by Yiannis Psychopedis.

8 Museum of Greek Musical Instruments

MAP K4 ▪ Diogenous 1–3 ▪ 210 325 0198 ▪ 8am–3pm Tue–Sun ▪ www.instruments-museum.gr

At this unassuming museum, you can see and hear the Middle Eastern and European influences on Greek music, and how Greeks transformed them into something of their own. The instruments themselves are beautiful, often intricately inlaid with silver, ivory and tortoise-shell. There are occasional courtyard performances (see also p54).

Temple of Olympian Zeus

Entrance to Mitropoli

9 Mitropoli
MAP K3 ■ Plateia Mitropoleos
■ 6:30am–8pm daily

Lavishly appointed, Athens Cathedral is one of the city's best-known landmarks. The archbishop of Greece (arguably the nation's most influential person) gives addresses here, and it is regularly packed for Athens' high-society weddings. Of greater artistic importance, though, is tiny Panagia Gorgoepikoos ("little Metropoli"), next door. This 12th-century church is built of Roman and Byzantine marble relics, depicting ancient feasts (see also p57).

Filopappos Hill

10 Filopappos Hill
Next to the Acropolis rock, pine-and-cypress-clad Filopappos Hill offers a cool, green place to stroll. The peak, marked by the tomb and monument of Roman senator Gaius Julius Antiochus Filopappos, offers sweeping views from the Acropolis to the sea. In summer, the Dora Stratou Dance Troupe puts on nightly performances of Greek folk dances in a theatre nestled among the pines (see also pp34–5).

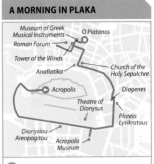

A MORNING IN PLAKA

Museum of Greek Musical Instruments
O Platanos
Roman Forum
Tower of the Winds
Anafiotika
Church of the Holy Sepulchre
Acropolis
Diogenes
Theatre of Dionysus
Plateia Lysikratous
Dionysiou Areopagitou
Acropolis Museum

▶ EARLY MORNING

Hike up to the **Acropolis** (see p77) early, to beat the heat and the worst of the crowds. Spend an hour or so admiring the temples.

Come down from the Acropolis and turn left onto the **Dionysiou Areopagitou walkway** (see p60). Your Acropolis ticket gives you free entry into the **Theatre of Dionysus**, where many great classical dramas were first staged.

Head back out to the walkway to visit the **Acropolis Museum** (see p77). Next, head to **Plateia Lysikratous**, named after the unusual monument to the winner of a 335 BC choral competition.

Stop for a frappé in one of the leafy cafés nearby – **Diogenes** (see p83) has great views.

LATE MORNING

From the square, head up to the charming 19th-century quarter of **Anafiotika** (see p77) to explore its twisting alleys.

Leave by Prytaneiou, stopping in the quiet garden of the Byzantine **Church of the Holy Sepulchre** (see p80), and lighting a candle from its famed holy flame.

From Prytaneiou, turn right on Mnisikleous and left on Kyristou for a choice of either the **Museum of Greek Musical Instruments** or the **Roman Forum and Tower of the Winds** (see p77). Finally, head back a block to **O Platanos** (see p83), for a hefty Greek lunch under a huge plane tree.

See map on p76 ←

The Best of the Rest

1 Kanellopoulos Museum
MAP J4 ▪ Theorias 12 ▪ 210 321 2313 ▪ 8am–3pm Tue–Sun ▪ Adm

A miscellany of high-quality antiquities on display in a Neo-Classical mansion.

2 Lalaounis Museum
MAP J5 ▪ Kallisperi 12 & Karyatidon ▪ 210 922 1044 ▪ 9am–3pm Tue–Sat, 11am–4pm Sun ▪ Adm (free Sat)

Jeweller Ilias Lalaounis showcases his creations at this museum.

Lalaounis Museum

3 Church of the Holy Sepulchre
MAP K4 ▪ Between Prytaneiou and Erotokritou

Miracles are associated with this beautiful Byzantine church, and many flock here at Easter to light candles from the holy flame.

4 Church of Agia Ekaterini
MAP L5 ▪ Off Plateia Lysikratous

The columns of an ancient temple still stand beneath the courtyard of this lovely Byzantine church.

5 Choregic Monument of Lysikrates
MAP L5 ▪ Plateia Lysikratous

Built in 335 BC, this monument honours Lysikrates, victor in the Dionysian Choral competition (see p42).

6 The Bath House of the Winds
MAP K4 ▪ Kyristou 8 ▪ 210 324 5957 ▪ 8am–3pm Mon, Wed–Sun ▪ Adm

A refurbished Turkish bath house from the 15th century, this small museum transports you back to a former era.

7 Frissiras Museum of Contemporary European Painting
MAP L4 ▪ Monis Asteriou Tsagari 3 & 7 ▪ 210 323 4678 ▪ 10am–5pm Wed–Fri, 11am–5pm Sat & Sun ▪ Adm ▪ www.frissirasmuseum.com

A museum of over 3,000 works of top post-war Greek and European artists.

8 Church of the Holy Trinity
MAP L4 ▪ Filellinon

The largest medieval church in the city was built in 1031 and is now Athens' Russian Orthodox church.

9 Museum of Greek Children's Art
MAP L4 ▪ Kodrou 9 ▪ 210 331 2621 ▪ Sep–Jul: 10am–2pm Tue–Sat, 11am–2pm Sun ▪ Closed Aug ▪ Adm

Admire works by young artists living in mountain tribes, cities and refugee centres. Many activities for kids.

10 Jewish Museum
MAP L4 ▪ Nikis 39 ▪ 210 322 5582 ▪ 9am–2:30pm Mon–Fri, 10am–2pm Sun ▪ Adm ▪ www.jewishmuseum.gr

The collection's 15,000 items tell the story of the Jews in Greece.

Exhibit at the Jewish Museum

Souvenirs and Gifts

Arts and crafts objects for sale at Forget Me Not

1 Centre of Hellenic Tradition
MAP K3 ■ Mitropoleos 59

A cavernous warehouse of Greek handicrafts. If you only have time for one souvenir stop, make this it.

2 Ioanna Kourbela
MAP C4 ■ Adrianou 109

Youthful, fluid clothes made from natural organic fabrics such as cotton, linen, wool and silk.

3 Pagani
MAP C4 ■ Pandrosou 59

This colourful shop of handmade decorative arts features an array of crafts and jewellery reflecting Greek tradition and culture.

4 Kori
MAP K3 ■ Mitropoleos 13 & Voulis

This little shop sells a select choice of gifts, including signed and numbered artworks by some of the country's latest talents.

5 The Athens Gallery
MAP C4 ■ Pandrosou 14

With branches in Athens and Santorini, this gallery represents both Greek and foreign artists. All the sculptures and fine art pieces explore Greek lifestyle and culture.

6 Forget Me Not
MAP C4 ■ Adrianou 100

This tiny gift shop is packed with unusual items by contemporary Greek designers, including T-shirts, ceramics and jewellery.

7 O Brettos
MAP L4 ■ Kydathinaion 41

Pop in for a bottle of this distillery's fiery home-made ouzo, and stay to sip a shot of surprisingly sweet *mestiha* and admire the huge barrels under the eaves (see p82).

8 Olive Tree Store
MAP C4 ■ Adrianou 67

This family-run store stocks bowls, spoons and chopping boards made from olive wood. They will also arrange shipping.

9 Lalaounis Museum Jewellery Shop
MAP J5 ■ Corner of Karyatidon & Kallisperi 12

Some of the world's most glamorous gold creations are to be found at Ilias Lalounis' celebrated jewellery house.

10 ArtShot
MAP K6 ■ Lempesi 11

This shop on arty Lebesi street offers jewellery, clothing and accessories by Greek artists.

See map on p76

Cafés and Bars

1 Klepsydra
MAP K4 ■ Thrasyvoulou

This tiny, quiet bar-café located behind the Tower of the Winds is surrounded by flower pots and pastel-hued buildings.

2 Melina
MAP K4 ■ Lyssiou 22, Aerides

This pink-and-gilt shrine to the late Greek actress and national heroine Melina Mercouri was once her favourite café.

3 Couleur Locale
MAP J3 ■ Normanou 3

This rooftop bar serves excellent coffee and other drinks, and offers one of the most stunning views of the Acropolis in Plaka.

4 O Brettos
MAP L4 ■ Kydathinaion 41

The walls here are lined with bottles of home-made, brilliantly coloured liquors that glow like stained-glass windows. The drinks are good, too.

5 Acropolis Museum Café
MAP C5 ■ Dionysiou Areopagitou 15

Located on the museum's second floor, this café-restaurant serves a traditional Greek breakfast until noon, with drinks and meals after that, on a terrace looking up to the Acropolis. There is free admission at the ticket desk for those coming just for the café.

6 Yiasemi, Plaka
MAP K4 ■ Mnisikleous 23

With tables on the stone steps below the Acropolis, Yiasemi serves home-made cakes and desserts. There's a fireplace indoors in winter.

7 TAF-The Art Foundation
MAP B4 ■ Normanou 5

This multi-purpose art and culture space is housed in a beautiful 19th-century building, and has a convivial bar-café located in the inner courtyard. It can be hard to find: look for the small wooden door.

8 7 Food Sins
MAP L4 ■ Plateia Filomousou Etarias 1, Plaka

Enjoy creative contemporary cuisine in a Neo-Classical building of 1911 or at the tables out front.

9 Vryssaki
MAP J3 ■ Vrysakiou 17, Plaka

An arts venue and bar, with rooftop terrace, Vryssaki encourages all sorts of experimental, artistic and creative activities, as well as hosting a range of cultural events.

10 Hitchcocktales
MAP K6 ■ Porinou 10, Makrigianni

Set in a refurbished industrial space, this place serves food and drinks with menu names inspired by Alfred Hitchcock's films.

Acropolis Museum Café

Restaurants and Tavernas

 1 O Platanos
MAP K4 ▪ Diogenous 4
▪ 210 322 0666 ▪ Closed Sun
▪ No credit cards ▪ €

Eat grilled or oven-baked meat accompanied by *chorta* (spinach-like greens), and enjoy the authentic taverna atmosphere.

Cod dish at Bakaliarakia tou Damigou

2 Bakaliarakia tou Damigou
MAP L4 ▪ Kydathinaion 41
(basement) ▪ 210 322 5084 ▪ Closed Mon ▪ No credit cards ▪ €

This family run local favourite has been serving up fried cod with garlic sauce for 145 years.

3 Mani Mani
MAP C6 ▪ Falirou
10 ▪ 210 921 8180 ▪ €

A spiral staircase leads to modern dining rooms with just a hint of rustic style. On the menu is Greek nouvelle cuisine.

4 Strofi
MAP B5 ▪ Rovertou Galli 25
▪ 210 921 4130 ▪ €

Strofi offers great rooftop views and food that is a cut above the typical taverna fare. Often draws theatre types from the nearby Herodes Atticus.

 5 To Kafenion
MAP K4 ▪ Tripodon 1 &
Epicharmou ▪ 210 324 6916 ▪ €

Located on a side street, this is often missed by tourists. Regional dishes are lifted with home-made sauces.

PRICE CATEGORIES

For a three-course meal for one with half a bottle of wine (or equivalent meal), taxes and extra charges.

€ under €40   €€ €40–€60   €€€ over €60

6 To Kati Allo
MAP K6 ▪ Chatzichristou 21
▪ 210 922 3071 ▪ €

Tucked in a small street behind the Acropolis Museum, this tavern offers delicious Greek comfort food.

7 Diogenes
MAP L5 ▪ Selei 3, Plateia
Lysikratus ▪ 210 322 4845 ▪ €

Athenian ladies who lunch head to this high-end taverna for its setting at the foot of the Acropolis, range of Greek wines and shaded terrace.

8 Dioskouroi
MAP J4 ▪ Dioskouron 13,
Plaka ▪ €

Despite being at the tourist heart of Athens, this café-taverna draws mainly locals, especially young ones, who come for the platters of *pikilia* (small bites).

Pikilia at Dioskouroi

9 Sholarhio
MAP K4 ▪ Tripodon 14 ▪ €

Choose from 18 different platters served on a giant tray, and wash your choice down with the house wine or some ouzo. Right under the Acropolis.

10 Tou Psarra
MAP K4 ▪ Erechtheos &
Erotokritou 12 ▪ 210 321 8733 ▪ €€

This established, pretty taverna has tables on the white-washed steps leading to the Acropolis. Try the *soupes* (cuttlefish).

See map on p76

🔟 Monastiraki, Psiri, Gazi and Thissio

For decades these old neighbourhoods of warehouses and workshops lay quiet, crumbling and neglected, enlivened only by the Monastiraki flea market, which spills out antiques, kitsch and junk from Plateia Avissynias. However, the appeal of a central location and some 21st-century ingenuity combined to create an authentically funky atmosphere. This part of the city is a hub for hipster clubs, cafés and restaurants. Gentrification hasn't robbed these districts of their character, though. Rather, craftsmen's shops and industrial buildings nestle side-by-side with edgy clubs, hole-in-the-wall Greek music dives and squares filled with outdoor cafés and bars. Adding to the mix are views of marble antiquities at the Agora and Kerameikos, Athens' greenest archaeological sites.

An exhibit at Technopolis

① Athinais
MAP A3 ■ Kastorias 34–6, Votanikos ■ 210 348 0000 ■ Museum: open 9am–10pm daily

A former silk factory converted into a trendy, upmarket arts centre. Athinais has a gourmet restaurant, a stylish bar, a music hall and an old-fashioned cinema. The centre also houses the Museum of Diachronic Art.

② Hadrian's Library
MAP J3 ■ 8am–2:30pm daily ■ Adm

Roman Emperor Hadrian built this sumptuous "library" (really more of

Hadrian's Library

a luxurious forum) in AD 132. It featured a marble courtyard, mosaic floors, concert areas and a small area for storing library scrolls, all surrounded by exquisite Corinthian columns (see p52).

③ Technopolis
MAP A4 ■ Peiraios 100
■ 210 346 1589

This enormous complex used to be a toxin-spewing foundry, hence the name of the neighbourhood, "Gazi" (gaslands). In 1999 it was converted into a huge arts centre, hosting top-notch exhibitions, concerts and arts spaces. The creation of Technopolis revitalized the entire area, making a name for Gazi as one of the liveliest nightlife hubs of the city.

④ Kerameikos
A green oasis in the middle of factories and hardware markets, this is the site of the oldest and largest burial ground in Attica. This

Kerameikos burial ground

is also the outer wall of the ancient city, and running through it is the Sacred Way. Outside the site, the road continues – still incongruously named Sacred Way despite its congested traffic and empty warehouses (see pp30–31).

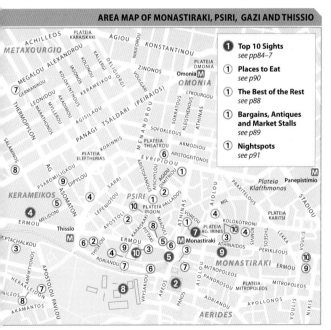

AREA MAP OF MONASTIRAKI, PSIRI, GAZI AND THISSIO

① Top 10 Sights
see pp84–7

① Places to Eat
see p90

① The Best of the Rest
see p88

① Bargains, Antiques and Market Stalls
see p89

① Nightspots
see p91

5 Plateia Monastiraki
MAP J3

There has been a church and monastery on this site since at least the 10th century. After most of the monastic buildings were lost during 19th-century excavations, the area was renamed Monastiraki – "little monastery". Built in 1678, the Pantánassa church, or church of the Dormition of the Virgin, is well worth a visit.

Plateia Monastiraki

6 Benaki Pireos Annexe
MAP A4 ■ Pireos 138
■ www.benaki.gr ■ Adm

In a renovated 1960s industrial building, this modern exhibition space stages temporary art shows, with an emphasis on contemporary photography, painting, sculpture, installations and architecture. Past shows include performance art and workshops by Marina Abramovic. The building focuses on a central courtyard, which is used for open-air summer performances.

THE JEWISH COMMUNITY

The area of Psiri and Kerameikos has been heavily settled by Greek Jews since the 3rd century BC. In 1944, the Nazis occupying Athens sent more than half the population to concentration camps; however, the community has slowly built up to once again become a centre of Greek Jewish life.

7 Plateia Agia Irini
MAP K3 ■ Aiolou St & Athinaidos

This popular square has lived many lives, from being a 19th-century business district to a flower market and even a garment district. Abandoned for a few decades, it regained its splendour and found a new identity as the city's buzzing hotspot for trendy yet traditional eateries, stylish bars and cafés that are located around its butter-coloured namesake, St Irene Church.

8 Agora and Agora Museum

One of the most interesting archaeological sites in Greece, the Agora is where Socrates "corrupted" youth, St Paul preached and converted his first followers, and the first decisions in the fledgling Athenian democracy were made. Don't miss the wonderfully preserved Temple of Hephaestus, or the recreated Stoa of Attalos, now home to the excellent Agora Museum (see pp16–19).

Covered walkway of the Stoa of Attalos, which houses the Agora Museum

9 Kapnikarea
MAP K3 ■ Kapnikarea & Ermou
■ 8am–2pm daily

One of Athens' greatest pleasures is walking down a crowded street and suddenly finding yourself face-to-face with a tiny, centuries-old monument in the midst of all the modernity. The beautiful 11th-century church known as Kapnikarea, smack in the middle of the shopping street of Ermou and beautifully decorated with mosaics, provides just such a moment. Built over the ruins of an ancient temple to a goddess, the church kept the theme, with its dedication to the Virgin.

Beautiful Byzantine art in Kapnikarea

10 Athens' Flea Market
MAP J3 ■ Plateia Avissynias & Ifaistou

Plateia Avissynias comes alive on Sunday mornings, when Athens' biggest and most colourful flea market fills the space and spills out to the streets around it. Here's where you'll find everything you didn't know you needed: pink cut-glass Turkish liqueur sets, old and ornate phones that still work, beautiful antique carved-wood desks, and piles of fantastic kitsch and junk. Use your haggling skills.

SUNDAY MARKETS

▶ MORNING

Start the day at the elegant **Café Avissinia**, named after the square it is located in, for an inviting breakfast and ambience.

Next, head for Psiri to **Melissinos Art** (see p89). Here, Stavros Melissinos will custom-fit you a classic pair of Greek sandals, and possibly try to sell you an English translation of one of his books.

Proceed to the historic church and monastery of **Plateia Monastiraki**, and then take a coffee break at **Athens 360**, a rooftop café and bar with lovely Acropolis views. Next, stroll towards the ancient halls and courtyard of **Hadrian's Library** (see pp84–5).

EARLY AFTERNOON

Head over to the **Agora**, the sprawling marketplace that was Athens' heart for centuries. Make sure not to miss the wonderfully well-preserved **Temple of Hephaestus** and the restored Stoa of Attalos, home to the excellent **Agora Museum**.

Now that you're warmed up, it's time to go back down **Adrianou** simply for the fun of haggling at the lively **Athens' Flea Market** at Plateia Avissynias. It's hard to resist buying at least something, though by this stage of the day it is more likely to be kitschy junk than bargain antiques.

Once you're done, retire with your booty to **Enastron** (p90) to enjoy a long lunch, while the marketplace closes down and the music and drinking start up.

See map on pp84–5

The Best of the Rest

Taverna on Plateia Iroon

1 Plateia Iroon
MAP J2

This square is surrounded by hip bars, old-fashioned tavernas and dirt-cheap student hangouts.

2 Museum of Greek Gastronomy
MAP C3 ■ Agiou Dimitriou 13
■ www.gastronomymuseum.gr

A museum dedicated to Greek cuisine, with temporary exhibitions focusing on particular periods or regions. They also run workshops and classes.

3 Bernier/Eliades Gallery
MAP A4 ■ Eptachalkou 11

This premiere gallery exhibits more international artists than any other venue in Athens, plus Greek artists.

4 Cine Psiri
MAP B3 ■ Sarri 40–44
■ 210 324 7234

This great outdoor cinema frequently shows black-and-white classics and foreign films (subtitled in Greek) during the summer months.

5 First Synagogue of Athens
MAP B4 ■ Melidoni 8

Before World War II, this area was the centre of Athens' Jewish community. The synagogue is the oldest in the city. Across the street, Beth-Salom Synagogue is Athens' main temple.

6 Athenaeum Maria Callas
MAP B4 ■ Adrianou 3

This conservatory, named after the formidable, world-famous soprano, hosts the annual Maria Callas Grand Prix opera competition.

7 Adrianou
MAP K3

The stretch of this street from the Thissio metro to Hadrian's Library has wonderful views of the Agora and the Acropolis.

8 Herakleidon Museum
MAP A4 ■ Herakleidon 16
■ 10am–6pm daily

Retrospectives explore the evolution of the exhibited artists via sketches, drawings and personal items.

Herakleidon Museum

9 Benaki Islamic Art Museum
MAP B3 ■ Agion Asomaton 22 & Dipilou ■ 210 325 1311
■ www.benaki.gr

In a Neo-Classical town house, four large exhibition rooms display Islamic ceramics, woodcarvings, glassware and textiles.

10 Herakleidon
MAP A4

Lined with cafés, bars and hipsters, this street feels both old world and fresh, and bustles day and night.

Bargains, Antiques and Market Stalls

 Bahar
MAP K2 ■ Evripidou 31
The whole area around the central meat market teems with old, family-run shops selling traditional foodstuffs. Bahar is one of the best-known for herbs.

 Artemis
MAP B4 ■ Thisiou 10
You never know what you might unearth among the books, coins, stamps, jewellery and antiques in this potential treasure trove.

3 Athens' Flea Market
Everything under the sun, from ancient coins to fake designer sunglasses, frilly knickers and genuine antiques at rock-bottom prices (see p87).

 D. Gounaris
MAP J3 ■ Ifaistou 21
This tiny alcove manages to stock a fine selection of traditional wooden *tavli* (backgammon) boards. Prices from as low as €10.

 Sigma
MAP J3 ■ Ermou 86
Purveyor of handmade wooden furniture and home accessories in styles that range from contemporary to retro.

 Pantopolion
MAP B4 ■ Ifaistou 9
This is the place to purchase traditional Greek foodstuffs – from Cretan olive oil and home-made sausages to yogurt with honey and walnuts made by the monks at Makariotissa Monastery in Viotia, plus a vast selection of Greek wines and local craft beers.

Martinos Antiques

 Martinos Antiques
MAP K3 ■ Pandrosou 50
This legendary three-floor shop gathers furniture, gold and silver, paintings, carpets, books and ornaments from all over the world.

 Melissinos Art
MAP J3 ■ Ag. Theklas 2
"Poet sandal-maker" Stavros Melissinos opened his shop of handmade leather sandals in 1954. He has now become a tourist attraction in his own right.

9 Aristokratikon
MAP L3 ■
Karageorgi Servias 9
Made from the finest Greek ingredients, these chocolates are strictly for connoisseurs.

10 Kalyviotis
MAP L3 ■ Ermou 8
Thread and fabric, bead- and button-filled shops populate the area around Ermou and Perikleous. Kalyviotis is the best one-stop haberdashery.

Sandals from Melissinos Art

See map on pp84–5

Places to Eat

1 Funky Gourmet
MAP A3 ■ Paramythias 13 & Salaminos, Gazi-Metaxourgio ■ 210 524 2727 ■ €€€

Quirky spot with a minimalist-chic upper-floor dining room, creating beautiful dishes from local produce.

Traditional interior of Oineas

2 Oineas
MAP J2 ■ Aisopou 9 ■ 210 321 5614 ■ €

High-quality, modern taverna food with a twist. Share a massive salad, then pass around bite-sized spinach pies and balsamic chicken.

3 Thanassis
MAP K3 ■ Mitropoleos 67 ■ 210 324 4705 ■ €

Athens' most famous *souvlaki* joint has been serving up hot, thinly sliced beef, with cool tzatziki, wrapped in pittas, since the 19th century.

Souvlaki in Thanassis

4 Mama Roux
MAP K2 ■ Aiolou 48 ■ 213 004 8382 ■ €

All-day café with tall windows and a menu inspired by European, American and Asian food.

5 Butcher Shop
MAP A4 ■ Persefonis 19, Gazi ■ 210 341 3440 ■ €

The butcher's-style interior includes a window display hung with sausages. Meat dishes are supplemented by generous portions of vegetables.

6 Ta Karamanlidika Tou Fani
MAP J2 ■ Sokratous 1, Monastiraki ■ 210 325 4184 ■ €

Set in a renovated Neo-Classical building, this tavern and deli serves Greek cheeses and cold cuts.

7 Aleria
MAP A3 ■ Megalou Alexandrou 57, Gazi-Metaxourgio ■ 210 522 2633 ■ €€

Come here for roast lamb with chickpea mousse and grilled fennel, followed by a range of Greek cheeses. The dining room opens on to a courtyard.

8 Athiri
MAP A3 ■ Plataion 15 ■ 210 346 2983 ■ €€

Relaxed yet refined. Creative dishes include orzo pasta with shrimps and fresh basil, and a salad of rocket, pomegranate, sunflower seeds, mint, prosciutto and cranberries.

9 Sardelles
MAP A4 ■ Persefonis 15, Gazi ■ 210 347 8050 ■ €

This modern taverna has outdoor seating and specializes in fresh seafood meze and good Greek wines. Try the grilled cuttlefish.

10 Enastron
MAP J2 ■ Mikonos 4, Karaiskaki ■ 210 321 6796 ■ €

Tucked behind the bars in Psiri, Enastron has a hospitable and warm ambience. Enjoy traditional Greek taverna fare.

Nightspots

Live music at Six D.O.G.S

1 Six D.O.G.S
MAP C4 ▪ Avramiotou 68

This cultural centre in the heart of Monastiraki focuses on visual art projects but also hosts workshops, live gigs, parties and film screenings.

2 Nipiagogio
MAP A4 ▪ Elasidon & Kleanthous 8, Gazi

This former kindergarten has been turned into a friendly club, with a fun vibe. In the summer, dancing moves outside to the courtyard garden.

3 Noel
MAP K2 ▪ Kolokotroni 59B, Monastiraki

A bar with a year-round holiday theme, and colourful interiors, Noel is famous for its fine cocktail menu.

4 Baba au Rum
MAP C4 ▪ Kleitiou 6

Sip exotic cocktails prepared with premium spirits, fresh juices and homemade syrups and liqueurs.

5 Hoxton
MAP A3 ▪ Voutadon 42, Gazi

Located opposite Kerameikos metro station, this hip industrial-style lounge holds art and photography exhibitions.

6 A for Athens
MAP J3 ▪ Miaouli 2–4

Open all day, this sleekly designed place offers views of Plaka and the Acropolis. Come for breakfast or an evening cocktail.

7 Underdog
MAP A4 ▪ Herakleidon 8

In a beautiful Neo-Classical building, Underdog serves speciality coffees, cocktails, local and international craft beer, plus brunch every day from 10am.

8 Bios
MAP B3 ▪ Peiraios 84, Gazi

With a ground level bar and a basement club, Bios stages alternative theatre and concerts. A café on the first floor is open all day, or enjoy your drink in the open-air rooftop bar with a view of the Acropolis (May–Sep).

9 Faust
MAP K3 ▪ Kalamioutou 11

Faust, with its black-and-red gothic style interior, is a venue for local theatre and live bands, and is also home to a lively bar and club. Music performances range from rock to jazz. Dancing takes over after 1am.

Trendy Booze Cooperative

10 Booze Cooperative
MAP C4 ▪ Kolokotroni 57

An arty club with exhibitions, videos and alternative theatre. Downstairs are magazines and board games; upstairs is loud rock music.

See map on pp84–5

🔟 Omonia and Exarcheia

Exarcheia and Omonia are among Athens' oldest, most well-worn districts. Though neither qualifies as beautiful, both are steeped in history, some of it quite recent. In 1973, the Polytechnic student uprising in Exarcheia was crushed by the junta, but it did eventually lead to the fall of the military dictatorship. The students left behind an area full of lively cafés; this is also the best place to hear rembetika, the gritty Greek blues. Below Exarcheia is seedy, clamorous Omonia, and just beyond is the colourful marketplace district.

Black-figure wine jug with a libation scene

1 Municipal Art Gallery

MAP B3 ■ Leonidou & Myllerou ■ 10am–2pm, 5–9pm Tue–Sat, 10am–2pm Sun

All of the best-known modern Greek artists are represented here, in addition to works by 19th-century Saxon architect Ernst Ziller. On display are his plans for the Neo-Classical National Theatre and for the city's grandest private homes, now mostly converted to museums.

AREA MAP OF OMONIA AND EXARCHEIA

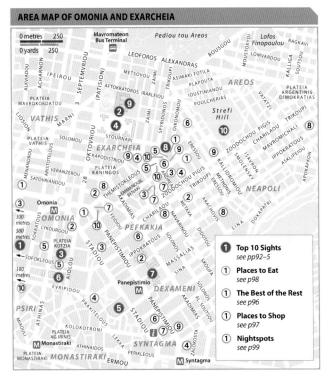

	Top 10 Sights see pp92–5
①	Places to Eat see p98
①	The Best of the Rest see p96
①	Places to Shop see p97
①	Nightspots see p99

Statue at the Polytechnic

4 Polytechnic
MAP C/D1–2

This is where the student demonstrations against the junta in 1973 (see box p94) began. In front of the Polytechnic there is a marble statue of a youth lying on the ground – a monument to the fallen heroes of the uprising. Every year on 17 November, all of Greece's politicians turn out to put flowers at the memorial.

2 Epigraphical Museum
MAP D1 ▪ Tositsa 1 ▪ 210 821 7637 ▪ 8am–3pm Tue–Sun

Housed here is a fascinating trove of Athenean lore. The collection comprises over 14,000, mostly Greek, inscriptions. The most important exhibits include a decree by the assembly of Athens ordering the evacuation of the city before the Persian invasion in 480 BC; a sacred law concerning temple-worship on the Acropolis; and a stele carved with accounts of the construction of the Erechtheion at the Acropolis in 421 BC.

Carved stele in the Epigraphical Museum

3 Plateia Kotzia
MAP C3

Lined with beautiful Neo-Classical buildings, this square is home to the Athens City Hall and the marbled National Bank of Greece. Next door to the bank is the more contemporary National Bank of Greece Cultural Centre, which was cleverly built to show off the remains of the ancient Acharnian Gate. Look out for the antiquities that were uncovered in the square, including tombs and part of an ancient road that once led out of the city.

5 Museum of the City of Athens Vouros-Eutaxias Foundation
MAP L2 ▪ Paparrigopoulou 7 ▪ 210 323 1397 ▪ 9am–4pm Mon–Fri, 10am–3pm Sat & Sun ▪ Adm

This was the first house built in Athens after it was declared capital of the new kingdom of Greece in 1834. Otto, the country's first king, had it joined with next door, and lived here while he waited for the first Royal Palace (now Parliament) to be built. Today the old residence houses a collection of paintings and furnishings telling the modern city's history, with a focus on the War of Independence (see p40) and the first years of the monarchy.

Nikolaos Gyzis's *Carnival in Athens* (1892), Museum of the City of Athens

Nut stall, Central Market

6 Central Market
MAP K1/2 ■ 7am–3pm
Mon–Sat

The enormous meat, fish and spice markets are a sensory overload that shouldn't be missed by any but the most squeamish. Several restaurants and even a *rembetatiko* dot the meat market, serving until dawn. Outside, the air around the spice stores, centred on Athinas, is redolent with vanilla, saffron and dried mountain thyme.

7 Athens University and Academy of Arts
MAP L/M1–2 ■ Panepistimiou

The city's university, the Academy of Arts and the National Library *(see p96)* make up a trio of the most important Neo-Classical

17 NOVEMBER 1973

The 1973 students of the Polytechnic are the great heroes of the modern Greek state. On 17 November 1973, they demonstrated against the junta, which had been in power since 1967. The uprising was crushed with tanks and guns but their courage eventually led to the junta's fall and the country's liberation the following year.

buildings in Athens. The column bases and capitals of the university entrance are replicas of those in the Acropolis Propylaia, and the Academy entrance draws from the eastern side of the Erechtheion. The university's frescoes depict the King Otto surrounded by personifications of the arts.

8 Plateia Exarcheia
MAP D2

It may seem a little worn around the edges, but Plateia Exarcheia is a lively spot surrounded by many cafés favoured by a left-wing crowd. The roads leading up to it are covered with politically charged graffiti and blanketed with leaflets advertising the latest demonstration. At the same time, the roads are fun to explore, lined with little independent shops selling all manner of records, vintage clothing and books. De rigueur frappé-sipping attire in

Athens University and Academy of Arts

the bars and cafés around here is unruly hair, black turtlenecks and messenger bags. At night it's an atmospheric place to be as the *rembetika* music and nightlife starts up.

⑨ National Archaeological Museum

This superb museum, often known simply as the National Museum, opened in 1891, bringing together a collection that had previously been scattered across the city. With its unique exhibits, including an unrivalled amount of sculpture, pottery and jewellery, this is without doubt one of the world's finest museums *(see also pp20–21 and p55.)*

National Archaeological Museum

⑩ Strefi Hill
MAP E1 ■ Anexartisias & Emmanouil Benaki

Strefi Hill is often overlooked by visitors due to its reputation as a druggie hangout by night. However, the hill is perfectly safe to visit during the day, where a short hike, popular with dog walkers, takes you up to a vantage point with spectacular views of the gritty neighbourhood of Omonia, Exarcheia, the Lycabettus Hill, the Acropolis and beyond. Just be sure to leave before nightfall.

A DAY AROUND OMONIA

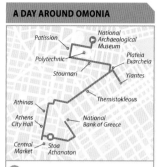

▶ MORNING

Start at Greece's greatest treasure storehouse: the **National Archaeological Museum**. Be sure to see the Mycenean Treasure, Thira Frescoes and Classical statuary.

When leaving the museum, turn left on **Patission**, noting the nearby **Polytechnic** *(see p93)*, scene of 1973's historic protests. Outside the building, a marble figure lies on the ground, a memorial to the fallen students.

Turn left on **Stournari**, and make your way to **Plateia Exarcheia** for a frappé and to watch the university students go by. In summer, head to **Yiantes** *(see p98)* for an alfresco lunch.

AFTERNOON

Venture downhill on **Themistokleous**. Walk quickly past the historic but chaotic and seedy Plateia Omonia on **Athinas.** Once beyond here you'll pass the stately **Athens City Hall** *(see p96)* on your right before turning left onto Sophocleous. Go down this street to see the **National Bank of Greece**, built on stilts over part of the Themistoklean Wall.

Double back to get to the city's real heart – the **Central Market**. Lose yourself in the sights, sounds and smells of the stalls. If it's not summer, finish up at **Stoa Athanaton** *(see p99)*, the city's best rembetiko, for fabulous music and a delicious traditional meal.

See map on p92

The Best of the Rest

1 National Theatre
MAP B2 ▪ Agiou Konstantinou
22–4 ▪ 210 528 8170

The majestic outlines of Hadrian's Library served as the model for this fine Neo-Classical building's façade. Performances by the National Theatre troupe are Greece's finest.

National Library

2 National Library
MAP L1 ▪ Panepistimiou 32
▪ 210 338 2503 ▪ 9am–8pm Mon–Thu, 9am–2pm Fri & Sat

One of the important Neo-Classical trio of downtown buildings (see p93). Venture in to admire the gorgeous reading room. The library is due to relocate in 2017.

3 Rebecca Camhi Gallery
MAP B2 ▪ Leonidou 9
▪ www.rebeccacamhi.com

This gallery presents both Greek and foreign contemporary artists. Visits by appointment.

4 Agioi Theodoroi
MAP K2 ▪ Plateia Agion Theodoron

A tiny, peaceful 11th-century church in the bustle of the marketplace. The wall paintings are 19th century.

5 Agios Nikolaos Pefkakia
MAP E2 ▪ Asklipeiou

Built in 1895, the church of Agios Nikolaos Pefkakia (St Nicholas of the Pines) crowns the top of steep Dervenion.

Church of Agios Nikolaos Pefkakia

6 National Opera
MAP L1 ▪ Akadimias 59–61
▪ 210 361 2461

The acoustics aren't great, but the loyal generations who have come in their furs and lacquered hairdos will always feel at home here. It is due to relocate in 2017.

7 Grigoropoulos Shrine
MAP D2 ▪ Tzavella

Teenager Alexandros Grigoropoulos was shot by the police in December 2008. Three days of riots ensued. A plaque, flowers and candles are dedicated to him.

8 Athens City Hall
MAP J1 ▪ Athinas 63

The headquarters for managing Athens' chaotic sprawl. The archaeological dig in front reveals an area just outside Athens' old city walls.

9 Odos Kallidromiou
MAP D2

Come to the colourful Saturday street market here for a real feel of the vibrant Exarcheia community.

10 CHEAPART Athens
MAP D2 ▪ Andrea Metaxa 25

A not-for-profit art space that hosts exhibitions by contemporary Greek and international artists. It promotes the work of emerging artists as well.

Places to Shop

Loumidis Coffee Shop

1 Loumidis Coffee Shop
MAP M2 ■ Panepistimiou 69

This vast corner coffee shop specializes in traditional Greek coffee, selling a selection of *brikia* (coffee pots) in which to boil it, cups and saucers, and sweet treats *(see p68)*.

2 Notos Galleries
MAP C3 ■ Aiolou & Stadiou

One of the few department stores in this country of small shops and boutiques, with an impressive range of local and international goods.

3 Stoa tou Vivliou
MAP C3 ■ Pesmazoglou 5 & Stadiou

In the commercial heart of Athens, this tranquil arcade with old-world charm houses bookshops, binders and antiquarian outlets.

4 Zoumboulakis Gallery
MAP M3 ■ Kriezotou 6

This celebrated art gallery and shop has a spectacular selection of original paintings and signed, numbered prints by many of Greece's finest artists.

5 CHEAPART Athens
MAP D2 ■ Andrea Metaxa 25

On the first floor of a Neo-Classical building, this gallery exhibits the works of emerging and established artists, bringing accessible work to a wider public. It organizes a major exhibition in December.

6 Eleftheroudakis
MAP M2

■ Panepistimiou 11

Seven storeys of English and Greek books, with an entire floor devoted to travel, plus a café, make this the perfect bookstore.

7 Zolotas
MAP M2

■ Panepistimiou 10

Celebrated for its intricate creations in hammered gold, Zolotas jewellery has long been one of Athens' most treasured brands.

8 Nakas Musical Instruments
MAP D2/3 ■ Navarinou 13 & Mavromichali

Five floors of musical items, from painted bouzoukia to violins, sheet music, DJ decks and loudspeakers.

Nakas Musical Instruments

9 Karavan
MAP M2 ■ Voukourestiou 11

Choose from the scrumptious baklava and *kataifi* at this tiny but deservedly popular alcove of a shop.

10 Music Corner
MAP C3 ■ Panepistimiou 56

A vast selection of Greek and East Mediterranean sounds, as well as classical music and jazz, blues and rock CDs.

See map on p92

Places to Eat

1 **Barba Yannis**
MAP D2 ▪ Emmanouil Benaki
94 ▪ 210 382 4138 ▪ €

There's no sign, but you'll spot this cult favourite by all the students tucking into hearty, dirt-cheap fare.

2 **Warehouse**
MAP D2 ▪ Mavromichali & Valtetsiou ▪ €

Choose from 30 wines by the glass, or 50 by the bottle, at this industrial-style bar. They also do coffees, light meals and a Sunday brunch.

The well-stocked bar at Warehouse

3 **Salero**
MAP D2 ▪ Valtetsiou 51
▪ 210 381 3358 ▪ €

Come to this eatery for tapas, Mediterranean dishes, cold-cut platters and fresh fish.

4 **Yiantes**
MAP D2 ▪ Valtetsiou 44
▪ 210 330 1369 ▪ €

Creative taverna classics – chicken with honey, raisins and coriander – served in a beautiful courtyard. Most of the produce is organic.

5 **Taverna Rozalia**
MAP D2 ▪ Valtetsiou 58
▪ 210 330 2933 ▪ €

Hipsters and locals flock to this *mezedopoleion*. The wood-beamed interior is ideal for winter; the courtyard, for lazy summer nights.

PRICE CATEGORIES

For a three-course meal for one with half a bottle of wine (or equivalent meal), taxes and extra charges.

€ under €40 €€ €40–€60 €€€ over €60

6 **AmaLahei**
MAP D1 ▪ Kallidromiou 69
▪ 210 384 5978 ▪ €

This relaxed spot features typical Greek taverna fare – from courgette rissoles to grilled pork fillet.

7 **Athinaikon**
MAP C2 ▪ Themistokleous 2
▪ 210 383 8485 ▪ €

Journalists trade stories at this beloved Athens institution. The plentiful mezes are consistently good.

8 **I Kriti**
MAP C2 ▪ Veranzerou 5 ▪ €

Cretan cuisine – *sfakiani* cheese pie, *kaltsouni* stuffed with cheese and honey, *apaki* (smoked pork) and seafood – at relatively low prices.

9 **Klimataria**
MAP J1 ▪ Plateia Theatrou 2
▪ 210 321 6629 ▪ €

In a seedy part of Omonia stands this warm, old-world taverna, which draws in guests with bouzouki music.

10 **Rififi**
MAP D2 ▪ Emmanouil Benaki
69A & Valtetsiou ▪ 210 330 0237 ▪ €

At this contemporary taverna, chef Eulis Panos comes up with ingenious twists on traditional Greek dishes.

Pastel-coloured interior of Rififi

Nightspots

Flowers aptly cover the walls at Floral, a spot for nightly events

 Floral
MAP D2 ■ Themistokleous 80

A legendary café hosting a variety of events, including concerts, exhibitions, bazaars, screenings, presentations and much more.

② **7 Sins**
MAP C2 ■ Themistokleous & Gamvetta 5

This club plays rock, industrial and Goth music, and stages fetish performances by international acts.

③ **Beatniks Road Bar**
MAP D2 ■ Koletti 14

Enjoy live blues music at this bar. The walls are decorated with various homages to beatnik and jazz culture.

 An Club
MAP C2 ■ Solomou 13–15

One of Athens' oldest and best-loved live music clubs, showcasing rock and alternative bands. Rave parties continue well after 1am.

 Stoa Athanaton
MAP J1 ■ Sofokleous 19 & Stoa Athanaton ■ 210 321 4362 ■ Closed in summer

Athens' premier rembetatiko, open day and night. Old-timers with cigars shower musicians with flowers, and, when the mood strikes, dance to gritty songs of heartbreak. It is wise to book ahead at weekends.

⑥ **Alexandrino**
MAP D2 ■ Emmanouil Benaki 69

A local favourite, this small French bistro is famous for its excellent wines and cocktails.

⑦ **Off The Chain**
MAP D2 ■ Zoodochou Pigis 25

This bar plays alternative rock, gothic and industrial music. It fills up late (after 3am) and parties till sunrise at weekends.

⑧ **Rembetiki Istoria**
MAP E2 ■ Ippokratous 181 ■ 210 642 4937

This bar, tucked into an early 20th-century building, has original moulded walls and ceilings. Patrons enjoy the earthy music.

⑨ **Mpoemissa**
MAP C2 ■ Solomou 13–15 ■ 210 383 8803

This is a great place to enjoy authentic live rembetiki music while dining on traditional Greek dishes. You can also just have drinks.

⑩ **Ginger Ale**
MAP D2 ■ Themistokleous 74

Decorated with flowered wallpaper and vintage posters, this café and cocktail-bar overlooks Exarcheia Square. It's a popular after-theatre haunt for actors who come to enjoy the sounds of soul and jazz over drinks.

See map on p92 ←

ⓉⓄⓅ🔟 Syntagma and Kolonaki

Plateia Syntagma, the centre of modern Athens, is crowned by the large, Neo-Classical Parliament building. Standing sentry outside are the *evzones* – soldiers marching solemnly back and forth in traditional short skirts and pompommed shoes. By Parliament, on the wide, tree-lined avenue of Vasilissis Sofias is Museum Row, where many of Athens' finest museums are concentrated. Behind Syntagma is posh Kolonaki, home to ambassadors, models, movie stars and the fabulous designer boutiques that cater to them. This is the prime spot for shopping, people-watching and glamorous but pricey café-sitting. Rising above it all is Lykavittos Hill, topped by a famous outdoor theatre, cafés and a restaurant with a view to die for.

Evzone guard in traditional attire

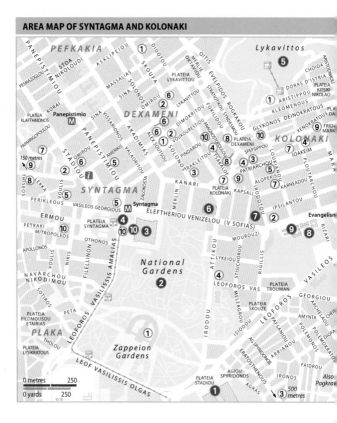

AREA MAP OF SYNTAGMA AND KOLONAKI

1 Kallimarmaro Stadium
MAP N6 ■ Vas Konstantinou
■ Mar–Oct: 8am–7pm; Nov–Feb:
8am–5pm daily

The formal name of this stadium is Panathenaic, but it's more commonly known as Kallimarmaro, meaning "beautiful marble". Built in 330 BC for the Panathenaic games, it later fell into disuse. In 1895, George Averoff had it restored with fine Pentelic marble, and it hosted the first modern Olympics in 1896. In 2004, it provided the final circuit for the Olympic Marathon and also hosted the archery competition.

2 National Gardens
MAP M4 ■ Amalias

The huge, shady National Gardens are an unexpected green refuge in parched central Athens. They were originally planted in 1839 as the Royal Garden of Queen Amalia, who had her horticulturalists bring in 15,000 domestic and exotic plants, many of which are still alive. The garden was opened to the public in 1923. It has a small zoo, a duck pond and a playground (see p61).

3 National Parliament Building
MAP M3 ■ Plateia Syntagma
■ Library: 9am–2pm, 5:30–8:30pm
Mon–Fri, 9am–2pm Sat

The imposing building was erected in 1842 as a palace for King Otto. Over the next 70 years, it suffered neglect, and in 1923, during a housing short-age, it acted as a homeless shelter. In 1926, after the return of parlia-mentary government, the building was gutted, renovated and re-opened as a single-chamber council for parlia-ment. Today it is the scene of debates that range from the surreal to the more mundane, viewable via a live video link. Its library can be visited.

National Parliament Building

4 Syntagma Metro Station
MAP M3

Syntagma station is as much museum as transport hub. When the city was busy excavating to extend the metro, archaeologists found thousands of priceless items on this site, which has been continuously occupied since Classical times. Many are displayed in the station, but the highlight is a glass wall overlooking the site, which includes at least two cemeteries (see p52).

Lykavittos Hill and the neighbourhood of Kolonaki

5 Lykavittos Hill
MAP F2

Steep Lykavittos Hill juts high out of Kolonaki, and the church at its peak is visible for miles around. Every summer, the Lykavittos Festival hosts a variety of top musicians from around the world in the theatre close to the church; there's nothing like watching Bob Dylan with the sun going down over Athens behind them. A smart café-restaurant nestles below the church. If you are very, very ambitious, walk up – otherwise, take the funicular from Aristippou.

6 Benaki Museum
The Benaki is one of Greece's pre-eminent museums, not only for its extensive and impressive collection of prehistoric to

Icon of The Raising of Lazarus, Benaki Museum

ZILLER THE THRILLER

When German King Otto was established as the first monarch after independence, he brought with him architect Ernst Ziller to rebuild the city. Ziller's Neo-Classicism can be seen in buildings such as the Cycladic Museum, the Numismatic Museum *(see p104)* and King Constantine's Palace – today, the official Presidential mansion *(see p104)*.

20th-century Greek art, but also because it's a lovely place to be. Among its highlights are the re-creations of Ottoman-style sitting rooms in 18th-century northern Greek mansions, and sumptuous Byzantine shrines. The superb books and jewellery in the gift shop and the rooftop garden restaurant are destinations in themselves *(see pp26–7 and p55)*.

7 Museum of Cycladic Art
Some 2,000 years before the Parthenon, a mysterious civilization on the Cycladic islands created the prototypical Mediterranean marble sculptures: simple, elemental female forms. The figures still resonate today, famously influencing artists such as Modigliani and Picasso. The Goulandris family, one of Greece's oldest shipping and philanthropic dynasties, displays the world's largest collection of Cycladic art in a beautifully restored Neo-Classical mansion. There are often exhibits by top contemporary Greek and international artists in the extra-swanky exhibition wing *(see pp22–3 and p55)*.

8 War Museum
MAP E/F4 ■ Vas Sofias & Rizari 2 ■ 210 725 2974–6 ■ 9am–4pm Mon–Sat

The two huge floors telling the history of warfare in Greece from prehistoric to modern times might not be everyone's cup of tea, but most will enjoy the Saroglos collection, including medieval suits of armour, duelling foils and engraved Turkish scimitars. Outside, there are several fighter planes and tanks – visitors are allowed to climb into the cockpits of most of them (see p55).

9 Byzantine and Christian Museum

The museum's vast collection dates from the 3rd to the 19th centuries, chronicling the rise and decline of the great Byzantine Empire. There are sculptures, icons and rich gold and silver religious trappings. The permanent collection is housed in a two-level space built partially under ground (see pp32–3 and p55).

Byzantine and Christian Museum

10 Evzones
MAP M3 ■ Changing of the Guard every hour

On guard in front of Parliament are the famous *evzones*, soldiers in the traditional attire of the rebels who won the War of Independence. It's hard to imagine fighting efficiently in this uniform: a short white skirt (with 400 pleats, symbolizing the years under Turkish rule), red cap and red pompommed shoes. The Changing of the Guard is like a slow high-kick dance. *Evzones* are selected from the tallest and most handsome men in the mandatory Greek military service.

AN AFTERNOON IN CHIC KOLONAKI

▶ MID-AFTERNOON

Start at **Plateia Syntagma** a few minutes before the hour to see the Changing of the Guard in front of the **Tomb of the Unknown Soldier**. Then head up **Vasilissis Sofias** to the **Museum of Cycladic Art** to ponder the mysterious prehistoric marble sculptures. Check out whatever temporary exhibition is on at the adjoining Stathatos Mansion – they are usually world-class shows.

Then it's on to **Plateia Kolonaki** for a frappé and a pastry at one of the cafés along the Tsakalof pedestrian way and some people-watching. The parade of wealthy wives, pretty playboys and Greek starlets provides recompense for the overpriced drinks – sip slowly!

LATE AFTERNOON

Afterwards, fan out from the square for some serious shopping or browsing of the shop windows and eyeing patrons at **Folli Follie**, **Boho** and **Twisted Classics** (see p105), as well as familiar international staples such as Gucci, Armani and Versace.

Towards the end of the day, go to the funicular station at the foot of **Lykavittos Hill**. Though close to Plateia Kolonaki, the walk is quite steep, so if your feet are tired you can take the 060 minibus from the square or a two-minute taxi ride. From the hilltop at dusk, watch the sky turn violet over Athens, while enjoying a drink at the café, or a truly special meal at **Orizontes** restaurant (see p107).

The Best of the Rest

1 Zappeion

MAP M5

The 19th-century Zappeion stands in pleasant grounds at the southern end of the National Gardens. Its tree-lined paths are open to the public, while the Zappeion itself hosts international conferences.

National Historical Museum

2 National Historical Museum
MAP L2 ■ Stadiou 13, Plateia Kolokotroni ■ 8:30am–2:30pm Tue–Sun ■ Adm

Greece's first parliament building, this is now a museum specializing in the War of Independence.

3 Gennadius Library
MAP F3 ■ Souidias 61 ■ 9am–5pm Mon, Tue, Wed & Fri, 9am–8pm Thu, 9am–2pm Sat

This library of multilingual volumes is among the world's best for all subjects Hellenistic.

4 Presidential Palace and Maximou Mansion
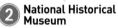
MAP N4 ■ Cnr of Irodou Attikou & Vasileos Georgiou

The former palace of King Constantine was designed by Ernst Ziller (see p102). Next door, Maximou Mansion is the Prime Minister's official residence – though incumbents sometimes prefer to live elsewhere.

5 Numismatic Museum/ Schliemann's House

MAP M2 ■ Panepistimiou 12 ■ 1–8pm Mon, 9am–4pm Tue–Sun ■ Adm

This coin collection is housed in the mansion of Heinrich Schliemann, discoverer of the Mycenae treasure.

6 Museum of the History of Greek Costume

MAP M2 ■ Dimokritou 7 ■ 10am–4pm Mon–Fri

Over 6,000 items of clothing, jewellery and adornments showing the variety of Greek dress through the ages.

7 Plateia Kolonaki
MAP N3

A pleasant square with plenty of cafés nearby where you can grab a drink.

8 Plateia Dexameni
MAP N/P2

Greener and lower-key than Plateia Kolonaki, and home to one of Athens' nicest outdoor cinemas.

9 Friday Morning Street Market
MAP P2 ■ Xenokratous

This is one of Athens' most lively fruit and vegetable markets.

10 Tomb of the Unknown Soldier
MAP M3 ■ Plateia Syntagma

A dying soldier, carved in 1930 on a wall on this square, commemorates Greece's war dead since the War of Independence (see p40).

Tomb of the Unknown Soldier

Chic Boutiques

The minimalist interior of Folli Follie

1 **Folli Follie**
MAP L3 ■ Ermou 19

Attractive, high-quality and affordably priced watches, necklaces, bracelets, bags and other accessories.

2 **Dassios**
MAP P3 ■ Vasilissis Sofias 35

Dimitris Dassios creates extravagant but tasteful waistcoats, kaftans, jackets, bags and jewellery from silk and leather, with ornamental details.

3 **Oikos**
MAP E4 ■ Irodotou 26

The most contemporary designs in Greece are showcased at this stylish store selling furniture, lighting and accessories.

4 **Twisted Classics**
MAP E4 ■ Irodotou 29

New collections of made-to-measure and ready-to-wear garments are created every month by owner/designer Katia Delatola using beautiful hand-drawn prints.

5 **Lena Katsanidou – Clothes & Accessories**
MAP P2/3 ■ Loukianou 21

Lena Katsanidou's Kolonaki boutique and upstairs atelier sells highly desirable items, including her signature line of bold, heavy-weight earrings fashioned out of silver and bronze.

6 **Graffito**
MAP M2 ■ Solonos 34

This retail emporium has a diverse collection of clothing, accessories and furnishings at fair prices from Greece and around the world.

7 **Boho**
MAP P3 ■ Karneadou 15 & Loukianou

Christianna Verouka is known for her upmarket 70s-inspired clothing – floaty scarves, chunky jewellery and leather shoulder bags – perfect for Greek island summer nightlife.

8 **Elena Votsi**
MAP N/P2 ■ Xanthou 7

A popular name on the international jewellery circuit, Votsi does chunky, rough-edged investment pieces that are worth every penny of their pricey tags.

9 **Kalogirou**
MAP P2 ■ Patriarchou Ioakeim 4

Stocks an overwhelming array of designer shoes and a wide selection of Kalogirou's own stylish creations.

10 **Bettina**
MAP N2 ■ Pindarou 40

Bettina's impressive stock includes international labels alongside Greece's own Angelos Frentzos and Sophia Kokosalaki.

See map on pp100–101

Hot Nightspots

Galaxy Bar, offering fine views and upmarket surroundings

Mommy
MAP M1 ▪ Delfon 4

This small bar and restaurant takes over the neighbouring pavements at weekends, as patrons spill out, drinks in hand.

Skoufaki
MAP M1 ▪ Skoufa 47–9

Small, dimly lit, smoky and full of artists and actor types, Skoufaki is Kolonaki's most famous, longest-established alternative café and bar.

3 Milioni Street
MAP N3

This street's fairy lights attract the chattering youth of Kolonaki until the early hours of the morning, as do the many bars and cafés, including Jackson Hall, an all-American diner.

4 Minnie the Moocher
MAP N2 ▪ Tsakalof 7

Set on Kolonaki's posh pedestrian strip, this 1930s-style hotspot serves a range of great cocktails, with jazz and swing music often playing.

5 Seven Jokers
MAP L4 ▪ Voulis 7

This café-bar aims to re-create the atmosphere of 1920s Paris. There are floor shows and huge sandwiches to absorb the vast amounts of alcohol served.

Galaxy Bar
MAP F4 ▪ Vasilissis Sofias 46
▪ 210 728 1402

On the top floor of the Hilton, this slick bar serves signature cocktails, sushi and finger food. At night, it offers stunning views over the city.

Rock 'n' Roll
MAP N3 ▪ Plateia Kolonaki 14

A popular lunch spot by day, Rock 'n' Roll transforms into a buzzing bar at night for a well-heeled crowd to party in.

8 Drunk Sinatra
MAP L3 ▪ Thiseos 16

This colourful and trendy vintage bar hosts a lively crowd that often spills out onto the pedestrian street.

The Clumsies
MAP K2 ▪ Praxitelous 30

Set in a Neo-Classical mansion from 1919, this popular bar with a wooden beamed ceiling serves great cocktails, light snacks and Sunday brunch.

Jazz in Jazz
MAP P2 ▪ Deinokratous 4

Notoriously hard to find (it's off Plateia Dexameni), this tiny bar has a jazz soundtrack, low lighting and a fine range of whiskies and beers.

Places to Eat and Drink

PRICE CATEGORIES
For a three-course meal for one with half a bottle of wine (or equivalent meal), taxes and extra charges.

€ under €40 €€ €40–€60 €€€ over €60

1 Orizontes
MAP P1 ■ Aristippou 1
■ 210 721 0701 ■ €€
Enjoy a view of the capital while dining on creative Mediterranean and fusion cuisine at the top of Lykavittos Hill.

2 Kiku
MAP N2 ■ Dimokritou 12
■ 210 364 7033 ■ €€
The original and best of the city's sushi restaurants. An impeccably presented, tempting selection.

3 Spondi
MAP E6 ■ Pyrronos 5
■ 210 756 4021 ■ €€
Upmarket French cuisine with Greek references – think foie gras, langoustine and milk-fed lamb. Tables are set in a courtyard garden and in three dining rooms with exposed stone and brickwork.

4 Kalamaki Kolonaki
MAP P2 ■ Dikastika 7
■ 210 721 8800 ■ €€
This casual, no-frills eatery is known for its Greek-style grilled meats. Try the turkey patties.

5 Winter Garden, GB Corner
MAP M3 ■ Vasileos Georgiou 1, Plateia Syntagma ■ 210 333 0000 ■ €€
Experience Athens' most elegant hotel without staying there, with a light lunch or afternoon tea.

6 Rosebud
MAP N1 ■ Skoufa & Omirou 60
■ 210 339 2370 ■ €
This former café is now a vegetarian restaurant. The menu includes guacamole, hummus, colourful salads and pasta dishes, plus vegan and gluten-free options.

7 Ratka
MAP P2 ■ Charitos 32
■ 210 729 0746 ■ €€
A Kolonaki classic, this restaurant is still a preferred dining spot for Athens' elite. It serves a global mix of dishes in refined surroundings.

8 Cookoovaya
MAP F4 ■ Chatzigianni 2a
■ 210 723 5005 ■ €€
Popular dishes at Cookoovaya ("owl" in Greek) include sea bass carpaccio with dill, and steak with mushroom ragout and potato purée. You'll find it close to the Hilton.

Dining room at Milos

9 Milos
MAP F4 ■ Vasilissis Sofias 46
■ 210 724 4400 ■ €€
At the Hilton, Milos serves creative Mediterranean cuisine with an emphasis on seafood and raw fish, with Black Angus fillet on offer for those who prefer meat.

10 Tzitsikas & Mermingas
MAP L3 ■ Mitropoleos 12–14
■ 210 324 7607 ■ €€
The "Cicada and Ant" serves reasonably priced Greek food. Try the three-cheese *saganaki* and stuffed pumpkin flowers.

See map on pp100–101

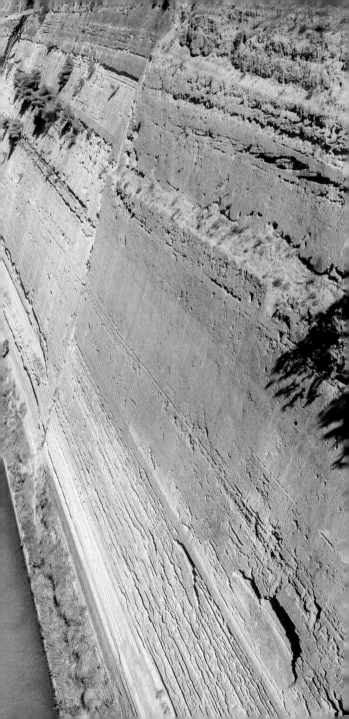

TOP 10 Piraeus

Renowned for seedy cafés, the city's port, Piraeus, is the gateway from Athens to the islands. The port of Athens since ancient times, it was redeveloped in 1834. Islanders from Chios, Hydra and Syros set up the first factories, joined by an influx of refugees from Asia Minor in 1922. It soon became Greece's main industrial centre, and is now the third-largest Mediterranean port. During the 2004 Olympics, cruisers served as floating hotels to boost the city's accommodation.

Hellenic Maritime Museum

1 Hellenic Maritime Museum

Akti Themistokleous, Freatida
■ 210 428 6959 ■ 8:30am–2pm Tue–Sat, 9am–1pm Sun ■ Adm

Housed in a 1960s building by the harbour, this exhibition opens with a map of Odysseus's voyage across the Mediterranean. It then traces the history of Greek naval trading, with models of ships ranging from the

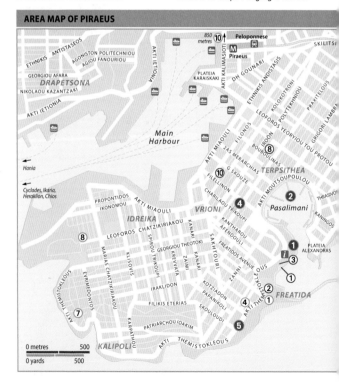

AREA MAP OF PIRAEUS

5th-century BC trireme (see p48) to modern tankers (Greece has the largest merchant fleet in the world). Naval warfare is covered by massive oil paintings of historic sea battles against the Turks.

Peace and Friendship Stadium

2 Pasalimani

This large bay, with a bottleneck channel opening out to the sea, is surrounded by tall apartment blocks. Inaugurated as Athens' main naval base in the 5th century BC, the ancient harbour of Marina Zea could accommodate 196 triremes. Today, up to 400 of the most impressive motor yachts in Greece moor here. It takes about 20 minutes to walk the perimeter of the bay, along a tree-lined promenade overlooked by open-air cafés.

3 Peace and Friendship Stadium
Off Tzavella Makariou

Close to Faliro metro station, this bowl-shaped concrete structure has hosted international competitions in basketball, volleyball and wrestling, and was a venue during the 2004 Olympics. It is also used for rock concerts.

4 Archaeological Museum of Piraeus
Odos Charilaou Trikoupi 32 ▪ 210 452 1598 ▪ 8am–3pm Tue–Sun ▪ Closed Aug and public hols ▪ Adm

Standing by the remains of the 2nd-century BC Theatre of Zea, the showpieces here are two classical bronze statues: the perfectly proportioned 5th-century BC Piraeus Apollo and the 4th-century BC Piraeus Athene. Also on display is a collection of 5th- and 4th-century BC marble stele (classical gravestones) with touching reliefs of the deceased.

Saronic Gulf

1 **Top 10 Sights**
see pp110–13

1 **Places to Eat**
see p114

1 **Bars and Cafés**
see p115

Archaeological Museum of Piraeus

5 Akti Themistokleous

From Freatida, a 3-km- (2-mile-) long coastal promenade, overlooked by apartment blocks and a string of informal fish restaurants, offers wonderful views across the open sea to the islands of Aegina and Salamina. The route, named after the 5th-century BC general and statesman Themistokles, who founded Piraeus, follows the course of the ancient seaward walls. Down below, a series of rocky bays offers the chance of bathing. The prettiest spot of all is Aphrodite's Bay.

6 Kastella

Built into the hillside of Profitis Ilias, which overlooks Mikrolimano, this picturesque residential quarter is filled with pastel-coloured Neo-Classical houses, built between 1834 and 1900, and a labyrinth of steep streets and stairways. There's a village atmosphere here, making it a great area to explore on foot. The highest point is crowned by the church of Profitis Ilias, which offers spectacular views of Athens, while nearby the small open-air Veakeio Theatre is used for staging delightful summer performances.

7 Yacht Club of Greece
Mikrolimano

Europe's top destination for yachters, thanks to its myriad islands, Greece has a 3,500-year tradition of sailing.

Yacht Club of Greece

Mikrolimano's bay

Set in landscaped gardens on a peninsula on the south side of Mikrolimano, the yacht club was founded in 1934. The main clubhouse is the province of members only, but you can stroll around the marina, then stop for a drink at the chic rooftop bar, Istioploikos (see p115).

Battleship Averoff

8 Battleship Averoff
Trokantero Marina, Palaio Faliro ▪ 210 988 8211 ▪ 9am–2pm Mon–Fri, 10am–5pm Sat & Sun ▪ Adm

Built in Livorno (Italy) in 1910, this 140-m- (460-ft-) long battleship was designed to carry 670 men in peacetime and 1,200 during war, and led the Greek fleet through the Balkan Wars and World Wars I and II. Negotiating a series of narrow ladders, you can explore the entire ship, from the kitchen and engine rooms to the main bridge, from the cramped dark space where the crew slept in hammocks, to the contrasting luxury of the officers' mess and the Admiral's sumptuous wood-panelled suite.

Piraeus metro station · METRO · Faliro metro station · Archaeological Museum · Peace and Friendship Stadium · Blow · Varoulko Seaside · Margaro · Pasalimani · Istioploikos · Mikrolimano · Moby · Imerivigli · Akti Themistokleous

▶ MORNING/AFTERNOON

From Athens, take the metro to Piraeus, then walk to the **Archaeological Museum** *(see p111)* and check out some of the ancient local finds.

Continue to **Pasalimani** and stop for a coffee at **Moby** *(see p115)*, overlooking the water. Take the time for a stroll around the harbour to admire the top-notch boats.

For a relaxed lunch, call at **Imerivigli** *(see p114)*, which offers fantastic sea views; otherwise, walk the seafront promenade of **Akti Themistokleous** for a reasonably priced informal feast of fresh fish at **Margaro** *(see p114)*.

EVENING

Take the metro to Faliro, then negotiate a busy main road past the **Peace and Friendship Stadium** *(see p111)*, one of Piraeus's venues that was used for the 2004 Olympic Games.

Continue south from the stadium to arrive at the pretty fishing harbour of **Mikrolimano** – less glitzy and more picturesque than the more central bays.

Here you'll find a string of waterside seafood restaurants, the best known of which is **Varoulko Seaside** *(see p114)*.

After dinner, either escape for a romantic nightcap at hilltop **Blow** in Kastella *(see p115)* or join the crowds at **Istioploikos** *(see p115)*, one of the café-bars with brash music and open-air seating on Akti Mikrilimanou.

⑨ Mikrolimano

Best known for its fish restaurants with open-air waterside terraces, this delightful circular bay is built on a human scale. The ancients believed it was protected by the goddess Munichia Artemis, and initially named it after her. The Turkish navy used it too, which is why it is still sometimes known as Tourkolimano (Turkish harbour). Today it is filled with the small wooden boats of local fishermen, who supply the surrounding restaurants from their daily catch.

⑩ Karaiskakis Stadium
MAP T2 ■ Karaoli Dimitriou & Sofianopoulou

Home ground to Olympiakos Football Club, this stadium was reconstructed for the 2004 Olympics and painted red in honour of its club's strip. With a capacity of 33,000 spectators, besides staging Superleague Greece and big international matches, it occasionally hosts rock concerts. It's also home to a small Olympiakos FC Museum. You'll find it next to Faliro metro station.

LION OF PIRAEUS

In medieval times the main port of Piraeus was known as Porto Leone in tribute to a 3-m- (10-ft-) tall marble lion that stood on the site of the present Town Hall. In 1688, the Venetians carried it off and placed it in the Arsenale in Venice. The respective city councils are now negotiating its return.

See map on pp110–11 ←

Places to Eat

PRICE CATEGORIES
For a three-course meal for one with half a bottle of wine (or equivalent meal), taxes and extra charges.

€ under €40 €€ €40–€60 €€€ over €60

① Varoulko Seaside
Akti Koumoundourou 52, Mikrolimano ▪ 210 522 8400 ▪ €€€
Michelin-starred chef Lefteris Lazarou serves delights such as squid with pesto, and red mullet in lemon sauce.

② Dourabeis
Akti Dilaveri 29, Mikrolimano ▪ 210 412 2092 ▪ €€
Since 1932, Dourabeis has charmed diners with its sublime fresh fish, simply grilled and dressed with lemon and olive oil.

③ Jimmy's Fish & the Sushi Tavern
Akti Koumoundourou 46, Mikrolimano ▪ 210 412 4417 ▪ €€
Waiters carry platters of smoked tuna and rocket, pans of lobster, and trays of fresh sushi to diners on the harbourside terrace.

④ Imerovigli
Akti Themistokleous 56, Piraiki ▪ 210 452 3382 ▪ €
Excellent seafood, but also a good range of meat choices, all accompanied by Greek wines, ouzo, raki and beers. Live Greek music.

⑤ Ammos
Akti Koumoundourou 44, Mikrolimano ▪ 210 422 4633 ▪ €
Located next to the sea, this casual *mezedopoleion* serves traditional meat and fish dishes.

⑥ Kapileio O Zaxos Komotinis
37 Piraeus ▪ 210 481 3325 ▪ €
This family-run taverna attracts both tourists and locals with its authentic and fresh seafood dishes.

⑦ Diasimos
Akti Themistokleous 306–8, Freatida ▪ 210 451 4887 ▪ €
Two blue-fronted buildings comprise this popular *ouzeri* and psarotaverna, which offer lovely views from the seafront terrace.

⑧ Margaro
Chatzikyriakou 126 ▪ 210 451 4226 ▪ Closed Sun dinner and two weeks in Aug ▪ No credit cards ▪ €
Diners here enjoy a rather limited but heavenly selection of fresh seafood including whitebait, mullet, bream and shrimps.

⑨ Papaioannou
Akti Koumoundourou 42, Mikrolimano ▪ 210 422 5059 ▪ €
Noted for its fresh seafood, the menu at Papaioannou also includes creamy home-made taramasalata, tender grilled octopus and barbecued sea bream. Round off your meal with *loukoumades* (fritters) drizzled with honey and cinnamon.

⑩ Vassilenas
Etolikou 72, Agia Sofia ▪ 210 461 2457 ▪ Closed Jul & Aug ▪ No credit cards ▪ €
A set meal of 16 mezes, served up in a steady stream to snack upon. There's a fixed price, and you are advised to book ahead.

Classy dining at Vassilenas

Bars and Cafés

 Moby
Marina Zeas, Pasalimani

Locals come here for coffee and cocktails, as well as views of the sea. Moby runs DJ nights at weekends, and it serves snacks, pizza and salads, plus Sunday brunch.

 Pisina
Akti Themistokleous 25, Freatida ▪ 210 451 1324

Centred around an open-air swimming pool, this modern bar-restaurant is stylish but relaxed.

Pizza at Moby

 RockFellas
Marina Zeas, Pasalimani

With walls covered by posters of well-known musicians, a bar lined with high stools, and leather sofas for lounging on, RockFellas serves draught beer and cocktails. It plays commercial rock till 3am at weekends.

 Blow
Idis 6, Kastella

For great views over the sea and back to Athens, walk up to Blow, on Profitis Elias hilltop, in Kastella, above Mikrolimano Bay. They serve coffee, drinks, cocktails and desserts, at tables both inside and out.

Cocktail at Blow

 **Mecca**
Akti Koumoundourou 62, Mikrolimano

Hot drinks, good food and cocktails can be had amid the modern architecture of this place with great views of the coast around Athens.

Bizz Bar
Akti Koumoundourou 8, Pasalimani

With sofas, pouffes and coffee tables on a wooden deck that goes right up to the water's edge, Bizz Bar is one of a string of lounge-cafés overlooking the flashy yachts in Pasalimani Bay.

Istioploikos
Akti Mikrolimanou
▪ **Open mid-Mar–early Nov**

One of the hip places to see and be seen, this vast rooftop bar commands a vantage point above the yachting marina.

 Small
Aristotelous 10

Artwork depicting famous fairy-tale characters cover the walls of this café. The evenings feature live music with famous Greek artists.

Adonis
Alexandrou Papanastasiou 57, Kastella

Located in Kastella, the most picturesque neighbourhood in Piraeus, Adonis serves snacks, fruit juices and coffee in the morning, and excellent food for lunch and dinner.

Troubar
Filonos 131, Piraeus

Run by five friends who studied film together, Troubar stages weekend concerts – soul, funk, rock and jazz – with free admission. The long wooden bar and warm red lighting create a cosy atmosphere, reminiscent of an old-fashioned cabaret club.

See map on pp110–11

🔟 North to Delphi

The landscape changes as soon as you reach Athens' northern suburbs; the sight of pine-clad Mount Parnitha opens the way to the varied landscape of central Greece. The region, Sterea Ellada, is fringed with mountains, lined with coastal towns and dotted with Byzantine monasteries and ancient ruins. Delphi is the country's most beautiful Classical site. Here, the fabled Oracle voiced its prophecies, telling Oedipus, among others, of his terrible fate. Delphi's surrounds are full of opportunities for swimming, trekking and skiing.

Picturesque coastal town of Galaxidi

AREA MAP OF THE NORTH TO DELPHI

Ancient temple ruins in Eleusis

1 Eleusis
MAP S2 ■ 210 554 6019
■ Bus A16 from Plateia Eleftherias
■ 8am–8pm Mon–Sat ■ Adm

For 1,400 years, this was one of Greece's most sacred places. Thousands of pilgrims took part in the Eleusian Mysteries, rites that celebrated Demeter, goddess of nature, and her daughter Persephone. Today Eleusis is a polluted industrial town, but there are still some scattered ruins, and an archaeological museum to help make sense of them.

2 Mount Parnassos
MAP R1 ■ Trekking Hellas: 210 331 0323 ■ Parnassos Ski Centre: 223 402 2700

Although developed in parts, Mount Parnassos offers splendid views, fine skiing and, in spring, wonderful trekking over wildflower-covered heights. The highest peak and most popular trek is the Liakoura. The truly ambitious can trek via Delphi by starting from Arachova very early in the morning, although this requires a guide. The best starting point for most hikes is the Greek Alpine Club refuge at 1,900 m (6,230 ft), 20 km (12 miles) north of Arachova.

3 Osios Loukas
MAP R1 ■ 10am–5pm daily
■ Adm

This is a contender for the most beautiful monastery in Greece, with its idyllic location, looking across a valley to the soaring Elikonas mountain range, and fine Byzantine frescoes within. The interiors of the two distinct 11th-century churches are covered in marvellous mosaic and marble icons and decorations.

Ceiling fresco, Osios Loukas

The mountain village of Arachova

4 Arachova

MAP R1 ▪ Tourist office: 226 703 1250 ▪ Several buses daily from Terminal B, stopping en route to Delphi

This mountain village makes a good base for visiting Delphi and Parnassos. It is a popular winter destination for rich Athenians, and room prices are higher here in winter. Though the main thorough-fare is lined with shops hawking local rugs, honey and cheese, the best way to explore is to get lost in its stone-lined passageways.

5 Evia

MAP T1 ▪ Chalkida tourist office: 222 107 7777 ▪ Train times and prices: tel 1110 ▪ www.ose.gr

Greece's second-largest island is so close to the mainland that you can reach it by bridge. There are several trains a day from Larissa station in Athens to Chalkida, Evia's central city. The spine of mountains running north to south and dotted with villages offers great weekend trekking, and if you go by car midweek you'll likely have its beaches and the thermal spas at the northern tip to yourself.

6 Thebes

MAP S2 ▪ Buses hourly from Terminal B ▪ Museum: Apr–Sep: noon–7pm Mon, 8am–7pm Tue–Sun; Oct–Mar: 10:30am–5pm Mon, 8am–3pm Tue–Sun ▪ Adm

This city was once one of the greatest Mycenaean settlements and home of the tragic dynasty of Oedipus. Next to nothing remains of the ancient sites, and the modern city offers little in the way of sightseeing, but Thebes is worth a visit for the Archaeological Museum, with its excellent collection of Mycenaean finds.

7 Delphi

This was considered the centre of the world, as Zeus divined by releasing two eagles from opposite ends of the universe and seeing where they crossed. Great mystic powers are associated with this site, whose jutting mountain, gaping chasms and rushing springs indicate a place of dramatic geological upheaval. In ancient times, priestesses communed with the Oracle of Delphi, which gave famously abstruse prophecies. Apollo won dominion over the Oracle, and the site is full of temples to the god and prophets (see p120).

Temple of Apollo ruins, Delphi

ORACLE OF DELPHI

The Oracle delivered divine prophecies through a priestess at the Sanctuary of Apollo. The priestess went through consciousness-altering rituals, which probably included chewing laurel leaves and poppies and inhaling the vapours rising from Delphi's natural chasm. She communicated the prophecies in a series of inarticulate cries, which priests translated into verse.

See map on pp116–17

Byzantine art in Dafni monastery

8 Dafni
MAP T2 ■ 210 581 1558 ■ Bus A16 to Eleusis from Plateia Eleftherias (30-minute journey) ■ 8am–3pm Tue & Fri

The lovely, domed, 11th-century monastery here, decorated with brilliant mosaics, is one of the greatest treasures of the Byzantine Empire.

9 Mount Parnitha
MAP T2

This beautiful mountain on the outskirts of Athens has many walking and trekking paths through its dense fir forests. In spring, its meadows are full of wild flowers. There are two refuges for climbers and a large casino-cum-alpine hotel, reached by cable car from the suburb of Thrakomakedones, and a good starting point for walks.

10 Galaxidi
MAP Q1 ■ Several buses daily from Terminal B

This chic, low-key resort on the Gulf of Corinth makes a great base for visiting Delphi. Located between turquoise waters and green mountains, it is tranquil and idyllic, except on summer weekends, when Athens' crowds pack the trendy cafés. Otherwise, take the time to explore its beaches and 19th-century mansions.

A DRIVING TRIP FROM ATHENS TO DELPHI

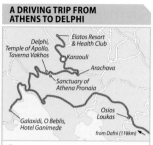

▶ DAY ONE

Set out from Athens, breaking up the three-hour drive to Delphi with stops at the monasteries of **Dafni** and **Osios Loukas** *(see p117)*.

Close to Delphi, stay either at the seaside town of **Galaxidi**, if it's summer, or in the mountain village of **Arachova** in winter. If the former, check into the charming **Hotel Ganimede** *(see p149)* and spend the afternoon at the beach; if the latter, consider a family chateau at the **Elatos Resort & Health Club** *(see p148)*. Here, you can take the afternoon to ski at the Parnassos Ski Centre, or to explore the many mountain trails.

DAY TWO

The next day, head to the ancient site of **Delphi** bright and early. Wander around the **Temple of Apollo**, considering the strange rituals of the ancient priestesses who communed with the Oracle. Be sure not to miss the **museum** or the nearby **Sanctuary of Athena Pronaia** *(see p120 for Delphi's sights)*.

If you are in a hurry to return to Athens, grab a snack at **Taverna Vakhos** *(p121)* in Delphi. If not, try the feta in filo pastry with honey at **O Bebelis** in Galaxidi, or the sausages and grilled formaella cheese at Arachova's **Karaouli** *(see p121 for both)*.

Sanctuary of Athena Pronaia

Sights in Delphi

 Sacred Way
This road retraces the route Apollo first followed to Delphi and ends at the temple dedicated to him. The view, of Mount Parnassos looming above and the plunging gorge below, is suitably humbling.

 Temple of Apollo
This temple contained the *omphalos* (navel-stone), marking the centre of the world, as well as the Oracle. Most ancient authors mention how rulers from all over the world sent envoys with lavish offerings to hear the Oracle's prophecies.

③ Sifnian Treasury
This temple-like marble structure, built by envoys from Sifnos, was the richest and most beautiful of several similar treasuries, all built as offerings to the Oracle. Its statues are now displayed in the museum.

④ Theatre
Built in the 4th century BC, this is one of the best-preserved theatres of ancient Greece. It also offers a sweeping view of the whole site, especially the dramatically varied landscape that makes Delphi feel so sacred.

 Roman Agora
This marketplace area was lined with stalls selling sacred objects, where visitors could buy last-minute offerings to the Oracle.

 Delphi Museum
2265 082 312 ■ Summer: 8am–8pm daily; Winter: 8am–3pm daily; Timings vary for Delphi site ■ Adm
The fantastic museum houses the greatest offerings brought to the Oracle from around the world.

Athenian Treasury

⑦ Athenian Treasury
The Athenians decorated their offering with elegant friezes depicting their hometown heroes Theseus and Herakles. The latter's famous Twelve Labours were performed at the Oracle's behest.

⑧ Sanctuary of Athena Pronaia
The sanctuary to warrior-goddess Athena was believed to protect the Sanctuary of Apollo from invaders. Though many of the buildings have been destroyed, those that survive are among the finest examples of ancient Greek architecture.

⑨ Sanctuary of the Earth Goddess
This rock circle around an opening in the earth celebrated the earliest deity associated with the Delphic Oracle: the earth goddess. The tradition of the Oracle and priestesses continued, but the ruling deity later become Apollo.

⑩ Castalian Spring
Though now mostly dry, this spring was where pilgrims cleansed themselves before entering the holy site. The elaborate fountain-house built around it is still visible.

Delphi Museum exhibit

Places to Eat North of Athens

PRICE CATEGORIES

For a three-course meal for one with half a bottle of wine (or equivalent meal), taxes and extra charges.

€ under €40 ■ €€ €40–€60 ■ €€€ over €60

① Taverna Vakhos
MAP Q1 ■ Apollonos 31, Delphi ■ 2265 083 186 ■ €

This family-run establishment cooks good taverna fare accompanied by views across the Corinthian Gulf.

② Epikouros
MAP Q1 ■ V. Pavlou 33, Delphi ■ 2265 083 250 ■ €

Traditional Greek cuisine can be enjoyed along with the magical views of the Gorge of Delphi at this friendly taverna. Try the oven-baked goat.

③ Kaplanis
MAP R1 ■ Plateia Tropaion, Arachova ■ 2267 031 890 ■ €

Flavourful taverna classics in a room with gilded chandeliers. In spring, try the fried courgette (zucchini) flowers. Year round, sample the *fromila* (barbecued cheese).

④ Taverna Porto
MAP Q1 ■ Akti Oianthis 41, Galaxidi ■ 2265 041 182 ■ €

Feast on large plates of cheap, tasty seafood at this waterfront taverna.

⑤ Karaouli
MAP R1 ■ Kalyvia Livadi, Arachova ■ 2267 031 001 ■ Sep–Jun: Fri–Sun ■ €

A simple, traditional and delicious taverna. Be sure to try the home-made spicy Arachova sausage and stuffed peppers.

⑥ O Bebelis
MAP Q1 ■ Mama Nikolou 20–22, Galaxidi ■ 2265 041 677 ■ €

Family-run O Bebelis serves Greek dishes such as caramelized stuffed onions, and pork with peppers in a cosy setting with an open fireplace.

⑦ Babis
MAP R1 ■ Kalyvia Livadi, Arachova ■ 2267 032 155 ■ Open for lunch Oct–Apr daily and for dinner at weekends ■ €

Go for a bowl of hot, aromatic *stifado* stew (see p66), as the crackling fire casts a warm glow over everything.

⑧ Lykos Winery Restaurant
MAP T1 ■ Malakonta, west of Eretria, Evia ■ 222 906 8400 ■ €€

Expect traditional Greek meat and fish dishes and fresh salads, plus excellent wines. Lykos also runs tours and tastings.

Taverna O Nodas

⑨ Taverna O Nodas
MAP R1 ■ On the main road to Livadia ■ 2261 025 422 ■ €

Just outside Livadia, with ample seating both indoors and out, Nodas specializes in roast meats – charcoal-grilled lamb chops, home-made burgers and tender steak – accompanied by colourful salads. Generous portions and good prices.

⑩ Thalassi
MAP T1 ■ Voudouri 13, Chalkida, Evia ■ 2221 023 539 ■ €

With tables on a waterside terrace, Thalassi is a pleasant place to dine. It's known for creative seafood dishes and favourites include grilled squid with couscous, pesto and sundried tomatoes, and a delicious shrimp and pumpkin risotto.

See map on pp116–17

🔟 Into the Peloponnese

Outside Athens, the Peloponnese is the part of Greece most steeped in myth and history. The Mycenaean kingdoms of Homer's *Iliad* were once believed to be merely legendary, until 19th-century German archaeologist Heinrich Schliemann unearthed their fabulous palaces on the Argive Peninsula. Now these sites compete with those in Athens as the most important in Greece. But, unlike Athens, the landscapes of those legends – the plains, where, according to Homer, great armies assembled, and the fields of Nemea where Herakles wrestled a lion to death – have remained the same for millennia, making this one of the most beautiful regions of Greece, as well as the most fascinating.

Statue, Ancient Corinth

AREA MAP OF THE PELOPONNESE

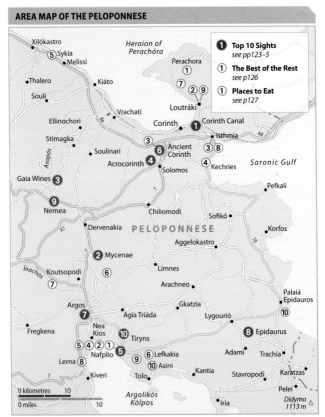

1 Top 10 Sights
see pp123–5

1 The Best of the Rest
see p126

1 Places to Eat
see p127

Corinth Canal

most powerful king during the Trojan War, commanding the citadel of "well-built Mycenae, rich in gold." And history confirms that indeed there was a Trojan War and a powerful civilization based in Mycenae. The evidence came together when Heinrich Schliemann discovered the palace at Mycenae in 1874, much of which accords with Homer's descriptions, including the wealth of gold.

Gaia Wines
MAP R3 ▪ Koutsi ▪ 2746 022 057, 210 8055 642 (call three days ahead for a tour and tasting) ▪ www.gaia-wines.gr

The Greek wine industry has gained international acclaim by bringing serious cultivation techniques to its sun-drenched soils and indigenous grapes. Gaia is one of the best vineyards, producing deep velvety wines from Nemea's Aghiorghitiko red grapes.

1 Corinth Canal
MAP R3

The isthmus connecting mainland Greece to the Peloponnese frustrated sailors for thousands of years, forcing them to make long, dangerous journeys around the peninsula. Everyone from Alexander the Great to Roman emperors Nero and Caligula tried digging a canal, but success came only in 1893, when French engineers dynamited their way through the rock. Boats take about an hour to make the 6-km (4-mile) journey.

4 Acrocorinth
MAP R3 ▪ 8am–3pm daily

This towering rock outside Corinth was the strongest natural fortification in ancient Greece. In Archaic times it was crowned by a famous temple to Aphrodite. The structures you see today are mostly medieval Turkish, often having been built over much older buildings. It is a strenuous hike to the top, but the effort is rewarded with great views.

2 Mycenae
MAP R3 ▪ Summer: 8am–7pm daily; winter: 8am–3pm daily ▪ Adm

Legend and history combine alluringly at Mycenae. Homer wrote of Agamemnon, Greece's

The rock of Acrocorinth

Colourful side street, Nafplio

5 Nafplio
MAP R3 ■ Tourist office: Martiou 25 ■ 2752 024 444

Small, seaside Nafplio is one of Greece's most beautiful towns. For years the Turks and Venetians fought for the city, leaving behind two hilltop Venetian fortresses and several Turkish mosques. The Greeks seized Nafplio when they won independence in 1821 and made it their first capital, before Athens took that mantle.

6 Ancient Corinth
MAP R3 ■ Archaeological sites: summer: 8am–7pm daily; winter: 8am–3pm daily ■ Adm

Corinth's location, between the Peloponnese and mainland Greece, made it a rich and powerful trading centre from Mycenaean times onwards. Material wealth was accompanied by a reputation for wild and licentious lifestyles, including polygamy and orgiastic cults, which St Paul addressed with great concern in the biblical Epistle to the Corinthians. After the 19th century, Corinth declined into a small, unattractive city. Its appeal resides in the extensive remains of the ancient glories, especially the 6th-century BC Temple of Apollo, and the Roman Agora and Odeon.

7 Argos
MAP R3 ■ Archaeological site: 8:30am–3pm Tue–Sun ■ Adm

Believed to be the longest continually inhabited town in Greece, the modern town sits right on top of the ancient one, leaving much to wonder about but little to see. The 4th-century theatre and excellent museum are well worth visiting; and, if you have a car, drive to the medieval castles of Larissa and Aspis overlooking the plain immortalized by Homer.

THE LABOURS OF HERAKLES

Herakles was fathered illegitimately by Zeus. Hera, enraged at her husband Zeus's infidelity, drove Herakles mad and caused him to kill his wife. In penance, he was required to perform 12 feats of heroism around the Peloponnese. He was cleansed of his sin and glorified for his feats, which, ironically, are attributed to the jealous goddess: his name means "glory of Hera".

Ruins of the Temple of Apollo, Ancient Corinth

8 Epidauros

MAP S3 ■ Summer: 8am–7pm daily; winter: 8am–3pm daily ■ Adm

The 4th-century BC Theatre of Epidauros is one of the best sites in Greece, marvellously preserved and with astounding acoustics *(see p72)*. Outside the theatre is the sprawling Asklepion, an ancient spa and resort devoted to Asklepios, the god of health.

Theatre of Epidauros

9 Nemea

MAP R3 ■ 8:30am–3pm daily ■ Adm

This was the site of the first labour of Herakles: the slaying of the Nemean lion. The lion's skin was impenetrable, so Herakles strangled the beast, then skinned it and kept its pelt as a coat of armour. This is one of several legends connected with the founding of the Nemean Games, which formed part of the Panhellenic Games. The highlight of Nemea is walking through the great stadium where the contests took place.

10 Tiryns

MAP R3 ■ Summer: 8am–7pm daily; winter 8am–5pm Mon–Sat ■ Adm

This was one of the most important cities of the Mycenaean civilization. Its fortifications of limestone were so massive that later Greeks believed they could have been built only by the giant Cyclops. Although not as grand as Mycenae, Tiryns is better-preserved, especially the ancient palace and great hall.

OVERNIGHT IN NAFPLIO

DAYTIME

Visit **Nafplio** on a summer weekend, buying tickets for a performance at Epidauros before setting off *(see p43)*.

Take a morning bus from Athens' Terminal A, having also booked a hotel in advance. The nicest place to stay is Nafplia Palace; Pension Acronafplia is more affordable but still good.

Spend the day exploring Nafplio's Old City. Buy some drinks and a snack, and take them up to the **Venetian fortress**, which affords glorious views of Nafplio and the Gulf of Argos. If you're feeling fit, climb the 999 steps to the top; otherwise, take a taxi.

Below the fortress, cool off at the small public beach. For more privacy, head down the walkway and go diving from the rocks.

NIGHTTIME

Dine at **Aiolos Tavern** *(see p127)*, returning to the bus station before 7:30pm, when buses depart for **Epidauros**. Even if the performance is in Greek, the powerful acting and magical setting will captivate. Programmes summarize the plot in English. Take the bus back to Nafplio and the hotel.

The following morning, check out, but leave your luggage at the hotel. Take the first bus to **Mycenae** *(see p123)*, whose tragic former inhabitants may well have been the subject of the previous night's play. Marvel at this legendary prehistoric city for a few hours, then go back to Nafplio and hop on a bus back to Athens.

See map on p122

The Best of the Rest

 Isthmia
MAP R3 ▪ 2741 037 244
▪ 8:30am–3pm Tue–Sun ▪ Adm

Much of the ancient site has been destroyed, but archaeology fanatics will still want to see the Sanctuary of Poseidon and the stadium that hosted the Panhellenic Games.

② Loutraki
MAP R2 ▪ Hydrotherapy
Thermal Spa: G Lekka 24
▪ 2744 022 215

Famed for its spring waters, Loutraki is a popular Athenian weekend destination. The top draw is the Hydrotherapy Thermal Spa, though the area is also home to a casino that's said to be one of the biggest in Europe.

③ Perahora
MAP R2 ▪ 8am–3pm daily
▪ Adm

Though little remains of the Temple of Hera, this is still an idyllic place to come and swim, with a wonderful lighthouse and chapel, and crystal-clear waters. Snorkellers can see ancient ruins underwater.

Turquoise waters at Perahora

 Kekhries
MAP R3

The site where Theseus defeated the Sinis, the giant who used whole pine trees to sling-shot victims across the water. Today the seaside town makes a nice stop on the drive to Epidauros.

⑤ Sikia
MAP R2

Along with nearby Xilokastro, this quiet seaside village is a great place to while away an afternoon swimming in clear water, eating freshly caught fish in tavernas scented with flowers, and drinking excellent local wine.

⑥ Heraion of Argos
MAP R3 ▪ N of Nafplio
▪ 8am–3pm ▪ Adm

This sanctuary to goddess Hera, built in the 7th–4th centuries BC, is a wonderfully tranquil spot, with great views over the Argive plain.

⑦ Skoura Wines
MAP R3 ▪ Piryelas, nr Argos
▪ 2751 023 688

Skoura is known for its white wines, especially its deep, fruity chardonnays – a rarity in Greece. Call a few days ahead to arrange a tour and tasting.

⑧ Lerna
MAP R4 ▪ 8am–3pm daily
▪ Adm

One of the oldest archaeological sites in Greece, with remains dating back to 4000 BC.

⑨ Agia Moni
MAP R3 ▪ Nr Nafplio

This 12th-century Byzantine convent and garden makes for a good day out. The nuns sell their own textiles.

⑩ Asini
MAP R4

This deserted Helladic settlement is a delightful swimming spot. Nobel Laureate George Seferis thought so, too, in his ode to a place "unknown, forgotten by all, even Homer".

Places to Eat

1 Kakanarakis
MAP R3 ▪ Vasilissis Olgas 18, Nafplio ▪ 2752 025 371 ▪ €

The menu here combines the best of Greek and Italian flavours. Delicious meze include courgette balls, tzatziki and moussaka.

2 Stavlos
MAP R3 ▪ Profiti Ilia 12, Nafplio ▪ 2752 306 702 ▪ €

Feast on freshly cooked courgette fritters and lamb chops at a table in the back garden. Stavlos is just outside Nafplio's touristy Old Town.

Marinos traditional taverna

3 Marinos
MAP R3 ▪ Ancient Corinth ▪ 2741 031 130 ▪ €

On the central square next to Ancient Corinth archaeological site, Marinos serves traditional Greek taverna fare.

4 Aiolos Tavern
MAP R3 ▪ Vasilissis Olgas 30, Nafplio ▪ 2752 026 828 ▪ €

Set on a scenic main pedestrian way in the heart of Nafplio, this family-run taverna is known for its service and delicious traditional taverna fare, from slow-cooked beans and grilled meats to stuffed vegetables.

5 Vasilis
MAP R3 ▪ Staikopoulou 22, Nafplio ▪ 2752 025 334 ▪ €

This taverna serves traditional Greek food in a fully air-conditioned dining room, but in the summer it is also possible to eat alfresco.

> **PRICE CATEGORIES**
> For a three-course meal for one with half a bottle of wine (or equivalent meal), taxes and extra charges.
> ·······
> € under €40 €€ €40–€60 €€€ over €60

6 Psalidas
MAP R3 ▪ Lefkakia, 7 km (4 miles) from Nafplio ▪ 2752 061 814 ▪ €

In the sleepy village of Lefkakia, east of Nafplio, Psalidas serves authentic home cooking in a pretty garden. Expect meaty stews, seasonal vegetables such as artichokes in spring and peppers in summer, and excellent local red wine.

7 Panorama
MAP R3 ▪ Agia Paraskeui, Perahora, Corinth ▪ 2744 079 155 ▪ €

Open all year, this taverna with distinctive stone and wood decor is renowned for its good food and convivial atmosphere, as well as its splendid views of the Corinthian Gulf. Live music and dancing on Saturdays.

8 O Kavos
MAP R3 ▪ Isthmia, 8 km (5 miles) from Corinth ▪ 2741 037 906 ▪ €

This tiny house by the sea serves up far superior fresh grilled fish than any you'll find in Corinth.

9 Rigani
MAP R2 ▪ Papanikolaou 5, Loutraki ▪ 2744 066 744 ▪ €€

With its innovative approach to traditional recipes, Rigani offers high-quality regional Greek food. Enjoy it in the cool garden, framed and shaded by trees and vineyards.

10 Mouria Restaurant – Gikas Holidays Club
MAP S3 ▪ Archaia Epidauros, Argolida ▪ 2753 041 218 ▪ €

The food here is rooted firmly in the Greek tradition: fresh locally caught fish, fine grilled meats and delicious home-made desserts.

See map on p122

🔟 Around the Attica Coast

From as early as the 5th century BC, the ancients built marble temples to their gods on verdant slopes covered in the dense foliage

of dark pines. This is a land where the legendary Theseus once roamed, freeing Attica from a scourge of monsters. Crowning the peninsula, at southernmost Cape Sounio, was the stunning Temple of Poseidon, sparkling like a beacon over the Aegean. Looking at Attica today, it is clear to see that parts of the coast have fallen victim to overdevelopment, but the jewels of Attica remain in the peacefully crumbling temples among the trees, in the best of the region's sandy beaches and in the ultra-luxurious summer clubs, which stretch further south down the coast every year.

Sanctuary of Artemis, Vavrona

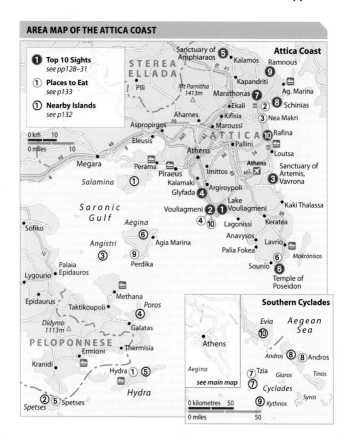

AREA MAP OF THE ATTICA COAST

1 **Top 10 Sights**
see pp128–31

1 **Places to Eat**
see p133

1 **Nearby Islands**
see p132

The picturesque thermal Lake Vouliagmeni, offering year-round bathing

1 Lake Vouliagmeni
MAP T3 ■ 210 896 2239
■ E22 bus from Athens ■ Summer:
7:30am–8pm ■ Adm

Bathers come year-round to take the warm, therapeutic waters of Lake Vouliagmeni, a large thermal spring that maintains a steady temperature of 22–25 °C (72–77 °F). The source of the clear, half-fresh, half-salt waters is still unknown, but devotees say there's no doubt about their healing properties. It's a great place to swim, especially on cold winter mornings, flanked by a high rock face on one side and trees on the other.

2 Vouliagmeni
MAP T3 ■ Bus E22 from Athens

A sprawling seaside resort suburb south of Athens, Vouliagmeni is lined with luxury hotels, yacht clubs and pricey pay-per-visit beaches. But the biggest draw for Athenians and visitors are the super-glam beach-side clubs, the centre of nightlife in summer. All are re-created in luscious over-the-top decor each year. Perennial competitors in the desirability stakes are Island, Tango and Spa.

3 Sanctuary of Artemis, Vavrona
MAP T3 ■ Markopoulo, Mesogia
■ 8:30am–3pm Tue–Sun ■ Adm

This temple to Artemis, goddess of the hunt and childbirth, was once the most sacred in Attica. Its highlight was the bear festival, where young girls dressed as cubs performed the "bear dance" in honour of the goddess's favourite animal. When King Agamemnon sacrificed his daughter Iphigenia to Artemis, the goddess saved her and brought her here, where she became a high priestess. Her tomb is the oldest cult shrine on the site. Today the site is well preserved and tranquil. Its museum displays cult finds.

Shopping in Glyfada

4 Glyfada
MAP T3 ■ Bus E2 or A2, or tram
T5 from Syntagma Square

Here, a wealthy, if somewhat overdeveloped beach-resort and flashy nightlife vibe prevail. There are plenty of designer shops and cafés to sit in while sporting new purchases by day, and trendy summer clubs to dance in by night.

Sanctuary of Amphiaraos

5 Sanctuary of Amphiaraos

MAP T2 ▪ 8am–3pm ▪ Adm

Built in the 4th century BC, this shrine was both an oracle and health resort. It honoured Amphiaraos, an Argonaut prophet tricked into fighting against Thebes, even though he foresaw that he would be killed. He was swallowed by the earth here, and reincarnated as a demi-god. In spring, flowers blanket the sight.

6 Temple of Poseidon

MAP T3 ▪ 2292 039 363 ▪ Bus from the KTEL terminal in Athens (2-hour journey time) ▪ Summer & winter: 9am–sunset daily ▪ Adm

The 5th-century BC temple is one of the few ever built to Poseidon. After

Temple of Poseidon on Cape Sounio

THE LOCAL HERO

Theseus is linked with Attica through a mix of mythology and enticing traces of historical evidence that suggest that a King Theseus may have actually existed. This king managed to unite the region's splinter states, while the reputation of Theseus the hero rests on tales of his slaying monsters and bedding everyone from Helen of Troy to Hippolyta, Queen of the Amazons.

watching the sunset from the white marble pillars of this ancient site on the peak of Cape Sounio, you may share the sentiments of the poet Byron. He asked the gods simply to "Place me on Suniom's marbled steep, Where nothing save the waves and I, May hear our mutual murmurs sweep, There, swanlike, let me sing and die." (See also p53.)

7 Marathonas

MAP T2 ▪ Marathon tomb: 2294 055 462 ▪ Museum: 2294 055 155 ▪ 8am–3pm Tue–Sun (for both) ▪ Buses daily from Mavromateon terminal ▪ Adm (for both)

In 490 BC, the Marathon plain was the site of one of history's most important battles. There, an army of 10,000 Greeks defeated 25,000 Persians, preserving the newly founded first democracy. A tomb to the 192 Greek soldiers who fell (in comparison to 6,000 Persians) still stands here. After the victory, Pheidippidis ran the 42 km (26 miles) to Athens to announce the outcome, then collapsed dead on the spot. A museum displays finds from the area.

⑧ Schinias
MAP T2 ▪ KTEL bus from the Mavromateon terminal

Many consider Schinias the most beautiful beach area in Attica, its white-sand coast hugged by dark pine forests. An artificial lake and an environmental park were built here for the 2004 Olympics, with many tavernas and hotels springing up on the once-pristine shore as a result. But it's still possible to find many lovely spots to swim along this part of the coast, especially mid-week.

⑨ Ramnous
MAP T2 ▪ 8am–3pm Tue–Sun ▪ Adm

The ruins of these temples to Nemesis (goddess of divine retribution) and Thetis (Achilles' mother and the goddess of law) are among Greece's most unspoiled sites, in an isolated and overgrown grotto. Wear rubber-soled shoes to avoid slipping on the stones.

Temple ruins at Ramnous

⑩ Rafina
MAP T2 ▪ KTEL bus from the terminal on Mavromateon

If you go to the islands of Andros or Evia, you'll spend time in Rafina, Attica's second-largest port after Piraeus. It's smaller and cleaner than its chaotic big brother, but still bustling, filled with fish joints and hawkers. If you have a few hours to kill, take the small bus from the port to the decent beach, which also has a bar. If you're brave enough, climb up on rocks abutting the beach and join the local children in adrenaline-rush-inducing cliff-diving.

A TOUR OF ATTICA

▶ MORNING

Start early with a drive out of Athens to **Marathonas**. Survey the plain where the Greeks won history's greatest military victory, and pay homage at the warrior's tomb. Then head to the ruins of **Ramnous**, focusing more on the scenery than the site's original purpose: praying for revenge.

Drive south down the coast, stopping in Loutsa for a grilled fish lunch at **Xypolitos** (Artemida Beach • 2294 028 342 • 12pm–2am).

AFTERNOON

After lunch, continue south to the **Sanctuary of Artemis** at Vavrona (see p129). From there it's a little over an hour's drive to one of Greece's most splendid sights: the **Temple of Poseidon** at Sounio. If it's still daylight, head to one of the two nearby beaches. The one on the left of the temple requires an athletic scramble down but offers scenic seclusion; the hotel beach on the right is accessible but covered with sun loungers. An hour or two before sunset, wander up to the temple, and watch as the marble columns turn to pink and gold.

Returning to the coastal drive to Athens, consider two dinner options. The nearby taverna **Syrtaki** or, closer to the city, Nobu's **Matsuhisa Athens**, in Vouliagmeni, where you can end your day with exquisite Japanese fusion cuisine and a romantic view of the Aegean Sea below a starlit sky (see p133 for both).

See map on p128 ←

Nearby Islands

 Salamina
MAP S3

Wooded Salamina has a rich history – playwright Euripides was born here, and in 480 BC, the Greeks famously beat Xerxes here. Its proximity to the industry around Piraeus makes it less popular today.

 Spetses
MAP S4

Popular with British tourists, Spetses offers pine forests, good beaches and a charming harbour town. Cars are banned, but fun water taxis can take you around the coast.

 Angistri
MAP S3

This tiny islet off Aegina has quiet beaches, clear beautiful water, a handful of small hotels and fish tavernas, and not much else.

 Poros
MAP S4

Overlooked by most tourists, Poros is famous for its fragrant lemon groves. Pass through Poros town to walk in the dark woods and bright groves of Kalavria.

Hydra
MAP S4

Lovely Hydra town, its cobbled paths winding among the old mansions around the clear-watered harbour, is one of Greece's most beautiful spots. Its popularity as a celebrity getaway hasn't dampened its charm.

Seafront at Hydra

 Aegina
MAP S3

An easy and rewarding day trip, only half an hour from Athens, with pleasant beaches, famously tasty pistachios, the Temple of Aphaia, and Agios Nektarios, one of the largest churches in the Balkans.

Agios Nektarios, on Aegina

 Tzia
MAP U3

Although only half an hour from Lavrio, Tzia remains peaceful and relatively untouristed. Its interior is fertile and flowered. Don't miss the stone Lion of Tzia, carved into a hillside, or the excellent local wine.

Andros
MAP V3

A favourite of Greece's jet set, golden-beached Andros is lovely, exclusive, and expensive. The Goulandris Museum of Modern Art holds world-class exhibits every summer.

 Kythnos
MAP U4

Mostly barren and less picturesque than the other Cyclades, Kythnos boasts the thermal springs at Loutra.

 Evia
MAP S1–U2

Huge Evia is the perfect island for hikers, with green mountains and long trails winding through inland villages. At the northern tip, posh resorts cluster around restorative thermal springs (see p117).

Places to Eat

PRICE CATEGORIES

For a three-course meal for one with half a bottle of wine (or equivalent meal), taxes and extra charges.

€ under €40   €€ €40–€60   €€€ over €60

1 Psaropoula, Hydra
MAP S4 ▪ 2298 052 630 ▪ €€

Family-run for several generations, this taverna serves traditional, good-quality Mediterranean food a few steps away from the beach.

2 O Psaras, Marathon
MAP T2 ▪ Leoforos Poseidonos 3 ▪ 2294 055 237 ▪ €

Enjoy fried squid, barbecued fresh fish and a Greek salad under big parasols on a wooden deck on Marathon's sandy beach.

3 Kavouri, Nea Makri
MAP T2 ▪ Marathonas Beach, Nea Makri ▪ 2294 055 243 ▪ €€

Top-notch taramasalata and grilled seafood (the squid is especially good) at this garden taverna by the sea.

4 Ithaki, Vouliagmeni
MAP T3 ▪ Apollonos 28, Vouliagmeni ▪ 210 896 3747 ▪ €€€

Elaborate cuisine and glitzy clientele in a wood-and-glass building set into a cliff overlooking the sea.

5 Patralis, Spetses
MAP S4 ▪ Kounopitsa, Spetses ▪ 2298 075 380 ▪ €

Patralis has probably the widest variety of fresh fish on the island and offers superb views of the sea.

6 Syrtaki, nr Sounio
MAP T3 ▪ 2 km (1 mile) N of the Temple of Poseidon ▪ 2292 039 125 ▪ €€

The most popular taverna around Sounio. The shaded three-storey seating area has a nice view of the sea, and the spit-cooked beef and octopus are reliably tasty.

7 Aristos, Tzia
MAP U3 ▪ Vourkari port, Tzia ▪ 2288 021 475 ▪ €€

A favourite of the yachting community. The menu features local cheeses, fresh fish and seafood. Reservations recommended. Open daily in spring and summer.

8 Endochora, Andros
MAP V3 ▪ G. Empeirikou, Andros Town ▪ 2282 023 207 ▪ €€

In Andros' car-free Old Town, Endochora serves contemporary Mediterranean fare in a white-washed shabby-chic interior. Try the pappardelle pasta ribbons with a beef ragout, grilled salmon with wild rice, and their signature salad, which combines lettuce, walnuts and dried figs.

Dining with a view at Nontas

9 Nontas, Aegina
Perdika, Aegina ▪ MAP S3 ▪ 2297 061 233 ▪ €€

Open all day, this beach-side taverna is famous for its fish and seafood, all caught by local fishermen.

10 Matsuhisa Athens, Vouliagmeni
MAP T3 ▪ Apollonos 40 ▪ 210 896 0510 ▪ €€€

At the Astir Palace Hotel, chef Nobu Matsuhisa presents his Japanese-Peruvian fusion cuisine. Seafood predominates, from his signature black cod with miso to sushi rolls and sashimi. Smart ambience, with stunning views over the Aegean Sea.

See map on 128

Streetsmart

Evzones at the Changing of the Guard

Getting To and Around Athens

Arriving by Air

Athens International Airport lies 27 km (16.5 miles) northeast of the city centre, to which it is connected by various means of public transport. The metro (M3, blue) runs directly from the airport to Syntagma and Monastiraki, in the city centre. In addition, there are four 24-hour bus services: the X95 runs to Syntagma; the X96 to Piraeus port; the X93 to the KTEL Kifissos bus station; and the X97 to Elliniko metro station (M2, red). Taxis are also available; the journey takes about 40 minutes and operates on a fixed tariff.

Aegean Airlines, the largest Greek airline, flies into Athens from most European capitals, including London, Paris, Rome, Berlin and Madrid, as well as from several cities in Australia, Canada, Russia and the Middle East. **Olympic Air**, now a subsidiary of Aegean, covers domestic flights within Greece. **British Airways** and **easyJet** fly in from the UK, while **Delta** flies direct from New York in the US, and **Air Canada** flies direct from Montreal and Toronto in Canada.

Arriving by Train

Greek trains are run by **TrainOSE**. However, the national network is quite limited – partly due to the country's mountainous topography – therefore, Greeks generally prefer to travel by bus rather than by train. The main train line runs from Thessaloniki in the north to Athens' Larissis train station in Kolonos, and is served by fast InterCity trains. There are daily international trains from Sofia (Bulgaria), and from Belgrade (Serbia) and Skopje (Republic of Macedonia) to Thessaloniki, so Athens is well connected to three of its Balkan neighbours by rail.

Arriving by Sea

Athens is served by the port of **Piraeus**, the largest and busiest passenger port in Europe. Each day, dozens of ferries, catamarans and hydrofoils arrive from the Greek islands, transporting both locals and visitors to the capital. Many cruise ships sailing around the eastern Mediterranean also dock at Piraeus.

For ferry timetables and booking, see the **Greek Ferries** or **Open Seas** websites, which cover all the main companies operating from the islands.

Arriving by Road

Major roads connecting Greece to its neighbours run to Thessaloniki: the E90 from Turkey, the E79 from Bulgaria and the E75 from the Republic of Macedonia. From Thessaloniki, the A1 motorway runs south to Athens (502 km/312 miles). To the west, Patras is connected to Athens (210 km/130.5 miles) by the A8. Drivers are obliged to pay at toll stations when exiting motorways.

Long-distance coaches from all over the country run to Athens, ending their journeys at either **KTEL Kifissos** (Bus Terminal A) or **KTEL Liosion** (Bus Terminal B), both located northwest of the city centre.

Getting Around by Bus and Trolleybus

Buses and trolleybuses, which are cheap but often very crowded, are operated by **Athens Urban Transport Organization (OASA)**. Yellow trolley-buses serve the city centre, while the blue buses run out to the city's suburbs.

Getting Around by Metro and Tram

There are three metro lines, operated by **Urban Rail Transport SA (STASY)**: the M1 (green) running from Piraeus to Kifissia; the M2 (red) from Anthoupoli to Elliniko; and the M3 (blue) from Agia Marina to Doukissis Plakentias, with an extension to the airport. The main nodes are the stations at Syntagma, Monastiraki and Omonia.

The same company operates three tram lines, forming a triangular network and connecting the city centre and the Attica Coast. The lines run between Syntagma, the Stadium of Peace and Friendship (at Neo

Faliro) and Asklipio Voulas (near the seaside suburb of Glyfada).

Buying Tickets and Travel Cards

During 2017, Athens' public transport ticket system will switch to electronic smartcards. Until then, tickets can be bought at kiosks throughout the city, and they are integrated to cover bus, trolleybus, tram and metro (but not routes to the airport). A single ticket costs €1.40 and is valid for 90 minutes from the moment you stamp it at the beginning of your first journey. A day ticket costs €4.50 and a five-day ticket €9. For the airport, a single express bus ticket is €6 and a regular metro ticket is €10. A tourist ticket is available for €22 and includes a round trip to the airport, metro, tram and bus for three days. There are reductions on some fares for those over 65, kids and students.

Getting Around by Taxi

Athenian taxis are yellow and among the cheapest in Europe. It is common practice to hail down a passing taxi in the street, but this can be difficult for foreigners, due to the language barrier and the gruff attitude for which Athenian taxi drivers are notorious. Visitors will probably find it easier to wait at a taxi rank (there's one on almost every city square) or to ask a hotel receptionist to call a taxi. Note that it's also normal for a taxi to pick up additional passengers

who are heading in a similar direction.

Getting Around on Foot

Athens' city centre is a joy to walk around, and all the main sites can be reached on foot from Syntagma. There is a slowly increasing number of pedestrian-only streets, meaning that if you pick your route carefully, you can avoid traffic altogether. The hilltops of the Acropolis and Lykavittos are often visible and can usefully be used as orientation points.

Getting Around by Car

Negotiating Athens by car can be intimidating even for the most confident of drivers. Due to traffic congestion and endless problems with parking, you are advised to do without a car during your time in the capital, though you may want to hire a vehicle for trips to the many sights beyond Athens on the Greek mainland.

  If you do have a car, try to choose a hotel that guarantees parking. If this is not feasible, there are several big car parks close to the centre. Most are located next to metro stations, two of the biggest being at Syngrou-Fix (Koukaki neighbourhood) and Kerameikos (Gazi neighbourhood) – though these are expensive and often crowded.

Getting Around by Bicycle

For years, the idea of riding a bicycle in Athens sounded absurd, but since

the onset of the economic crisis, more and more locals have bought bikes and started cycling around the city. However, there are no official bike lanes and car drivers still have a low tolerance, so take care while riding.

DIRECTORY

AIRPORTS

Athens International Airport
w aia.gr

AIRLINES

Aegean Airlines
w en.aegeanair.com

Air Canada
w aircanada.com

British Airways
w britishairways.com

Delta
w delta.com

easyJet
w easyjet.com

Olympic Air
w olympicair.com

RAIL SERVICES

TrainOSE
w trainose.gr

FERRY SERVICES

Greek Ferries
w greekferries.gr

Open Seas
w openseas.gr

Piraeus
w olp.gr

BUSES AND TROLLEYBUSES

Athens Urban Transport Organization (OASA)
w oasa.gr

KTEL Kifissos
Leoforos Kifisou 100
w ktelbus.com

KTEL Liosion
Liosion 260
w ktelbus.com

METRO AND TRAM

Urban Rail Transport SA (STASY)
w stasy.gr

Practical Information

Passports and Visas

Visitors from the EU (plus Norway and Iceland) can freely enter Greece with an ID card or passport – and stay indefinitely. Visitors from the US, Canada, Australia and New Zealand need only a valid passport for entry (no visa required) and can stay for up to 90 days. For longer stays, they must obtain a resident's permit from the Alien's Bureau in Athens. Nationals from most other countries need a visa and should consult the **Hellenic Republic Ministry of Foreign Affairs** website or the Greek embassy in their country of origin. Schengen visas are valid for Greece.

Travel Safety Advice

Visitors can get up-to-date travel safety information from the **Foreign and Commonwealth Office** in the UK, the **State Department** in the US and the **Department of Foreign Affairs and Trade** in Australia.

Customs Regulations

EU citizens are no longer subjected to export limits on alcohol, tobacco and perfume, as long as they are for personal use. Import limits for EU citizens are: 800 cigarettes, 400 cigarillos, 200 cigars, 1 kg of smoking tobacco, 10 litres of spirits over 22 per cent, 20 litres of alcoholic beverages under 22 per cent, 90 litres of wine (60 litres of sparkling wine) and 110 litres of beer.

Visitors aged over 17 from non-EU countries can carry in their personal luggage: 200 cigarettes or 250 g of smoking tobacco, 1 litre of spirits, 4 litres of still wine and 16 litres of beer. Note that there are strict limits on the import-export of antiquities, archaeological artifacts, firearms and weapons.

Travel Insurance

All travellers are advised to take out comprehensive travel insurance against theft or loss, accidents, illness, and travel delays or cancellations. Greece has a reciprocal health agreement with other EU countries, and visitors from the EU will receive emergency treatment if they carry a **European Health Insurance Card (EHIC)**. However, dental care is not covered. Visitors from outside the EU should check if their country has reciprocal agreements with Greece before travelling.

Emergency Services

The ambulance service, fire brigade and police can be reached on the **European Emergency Number**. There are also dedicated lines for each of these emergency services. In the case of a medical emergency, another option is **SOS Doctors**, a private organization on call 24/7, though be aware that its services are not covered by public healthcare.

Health

No vaccinations are required to visit Greece, there are few health hazards, and the tap water in Athens is of excellent quality. For minor ailments, go to a *farmakeio* (pharmacy). They are marked with a large green cross on a white background, and are open 8:30am–2pm Mon–Fri. In addition, they have a rotation system for working in the afternoon, at night and at weekends. If you go to your nearest pharmacy and find it closed, there will be a notice in the window giving the address of the next nearest on-duty pharmacy. However, the information is posted in Greek, so you might find it easier to call 1434, where an operator will be able to advise you on where to go.

The main public hospitals in Athens are **Evangelismos** in Kolonaki, in the city centre, and **Gennimatas** in Holorgos, a short distance east of the centre. **Hygeia** in Marousi, north of the centre, is a big private hospital.

Note that since the onset of the economic crisis and the imposition of stringent austerity measures, public hospitals have been severely underfunded and understaffed. Corruption has always been rife in the Greek healthcare system, and many doctors expect "under-the-table" payments in return for priority treatment.

Personal Security

Despite what is reported in the press, Athens remains one of the safest capital cities in Europe. While big public demonstrations and protest marches may look alarming, especially when the police fire tear-gas at the crowds, they are regarded as a normal part of Greek life. If demonstrations do turn violent, this normally happens at Syntagma Square, in front of the Parliament. If you don't want to be involved, avoid this area on days when strikes and marches are announced.

Athens has a low crime rate, though there has been a recent rise in pickpocketing, especially on the metro and crowded buses. Busy areas of the city are generally very safe at night. However, the neighbourhood around Omonia Square can be intimidating and is best avoided after dark, as it has become a magnet for drug addicts and marginalized communities, while Victoria Square, situated north of Omonia, has become an unofficial gathering point for refugees and immigrants.

If you do fall victim to petty crime, such as theft, or have cause to complain about shops, restaurants, tour guides or taxi drivers, you should contact the **tourist police**. Their job is to resolve problems relating to tourism, and they speak several foreign languages, including English.

DIRECTORY

PASSPORTS AND VISAS

Hellenic Republic Ministry of Foreign Affairs
W mfa.gr

EMBASSIES AND CONSULATES

Australia
MAP H2 ▪ Level 6, Thon Building, Kifisias and Alexandrias Avenue, Ambelokipi
C 210 870 4000
W greece.embassy.gov.au

Canada
Ethnikis Antistaseos 48, Halandri
C 210 727 3400
W canadainternational.gc.ca/greece-grece

New Zealand (Consulate)
Kifissias 76, Ambelokipi
C 210 692 4136
W new-zealand.visahq.com/embassy/greece

Republic of Ireland
MAP E5 ▪ Vassileos Konstantinou 7
C 210 723 2771
W dfa.ie/irish-embassy/greece

United Kingdom
MAP F4 ▪ Ploutarchou 1
C 210 727 2600
W gov.uk/government/world/organisations/british-embassy-athens

USA
MAP G3
▪ Vasilissis Sofias 91
C 210 721 2951
W athens.usembassy.gov

TRAVEL SAFETY ADVICE

Australian Department of Foreign Affairs and Trade
W dfat.gov.au
W smartraveller.gov.au

UK Foreign and Commonwealth Office
W gov.uk/foreign-travel-advice

US State Department
W travel.state.gov

EMERGENCY SERVICES

European Emergency Number
C 112

Police
C 100

Ambulance
C 166

Fire
C 199

SOS Doctors
C 1016

HEALTH

Duty Hospitals and Pharmacies
C 1434

Evangelismos Hospital
Ipsilantou 45–7
C 213 204 1000
W evaggelismos-hosp.gr

Gennimatas Hospital
Mesogeion 154, Holorgos
C 213 203 2000
W gna-gennimatas.gr

Hygeia Hospital
Erthrou Stavrou 4 and Kifissias, Marousi
C 210 686 7000
W hygeia.gr

PERSONAL SECURITY

Tourist police
C 1571

Currency and Banking

Greece is a member of the Eurozone and uses the euro (€), which is divided into 100 cents (*lepta* in Greek). Notes are in denominations of €500, €200, €100, €50, €20, €10 and €5. Coins come in denominations of €2, €1 and 50, 20, 10, 5, 2 and 1 cents.

ATMs (cash machines) are widely available and the easiest way to get cash. Surcharges depend on your bank. Alternatively, foreign currencies can be exchanged for euros at bureaux de change at the airport and at most banks. A passport or ID card is required when exchanging currencies.

Credit cards (American Express, Diners Club, MasterCard and Visa) are widely accepted, though smaller bars and eateries might not take them. If your card is stolen, inform the police and your credit card company at once.

Internet and Telephone

Many hotels, restaurants and cafés offer free Wi-Fi. Syntagma Square, in the city centre offers a free Wi-Fi hotspot. Internet cafés can be found throughout the city.

The dialling code for Greece is 0030, and Athens' city code is 210 and 211. Phone numbers must be dialled in full, including the city code.

Most mobile phones will work in Greece and roaming charges are being scrapped in the EU, from June 2017. Visitors from outside the EU can buy a local SIM card or a pay-as-you-go mobile phone to avoid roaming charges.

Postal Services

The main branch of Greece's **Hellenic Post (ELTA)** post office is on Syntagma Square and is open 8am–8pm Mon–Fri, 8am–2pm Sat and 9am–1pm Sun. Smaller post offices around the city generally work 8am–2pm Mon–Fri only. Letter boxes are bright yellow.

Television and Radio

There are three state-owned TV channels: ERT1 for news and current affairs, ERT2 for entertainment and sports and ERT3 for viewers in northern Greece. They are run by the Hellenic Broadcasting Corporation (ERT). In addition, there is a host of private channels airing soap operas, game shows, sport and films (mainly foreign productions, shown in the original version, with Greek subtitles). Most hotels have in-room TVs set on international channels such as the BBC, CNN and Euronews.

There are three main state-owned radio channels: ERA1, which offers news and current affairs; ERA2, which primarily plays music; and ERA3, which focuses on culture and classical music. There are also countless local stations, which play predominantly Greek music.

Newspapers and Magazines

Newsstands in the city centre stock foreign-language newspapers, though they are sometimes a day out of date. The main daily local newspapers are *Kathimerini* and *Ta Nea*, with *To Vima* a popular Sunday newspaper. *Kathimerini* also publishes an abridged English-language edition as a supplement to the *International Herald Tribune* in Greece, and articles in English can be found on the *Kathimerini* website. The weekly magazines *Athinorama* and *LiFO*, and their respective websites, offer comprehensive listings and reviews, as well as articles on local topics, but they are published in Greek only.

Opening Hours

Office hours are generally 8:30am–5pm Mon–Fri, with some businesses closing completely during August. Banks open 8am–2:30pm Mon–Thu and 8am–2pm Fri.

Shopping hours are more complicated. In the past, small, family-run stores worked 9am–2:30pm Mon and Wed; 9am–1:30pm and 5:30–8:30pm Tue and Thu–Fri; and 9am–3pm Sat. That is slowly changing to come into line with Athens' bigger European stores, which work 10am–9pm Mon–Sat. However, there are no hard and fast rules, and opening hours vary from store to store. Some stores close completely in August.

Most museums are open Apr–Oct daily (times vary from museum to museum) but work reduced hours Nov–Mar, opening Tue–Sun (closed Mon). Most archaeological sites are open daily (Apr–Oct: 8am–8pm daily and Nov–Mar 8am–3pm).

Most banks, stores and businesses close on public holidays. These are: New Year's Day (1 Jan), Epiphany (6 Jan), Shrove Monday, Independence Day (25 Mar), Good Friday, Easter Sunday, Easter Monday, Labour Day (1 May), Whit Monday, Assumption (15 Aug), Ohi Day (28 Oct), Christmas Day (25 Dec) and 26 December.

Time Difference

Greece operates on Eastern European Time (EET), which is two hours ahead of Greenwich Mean Time (GMT) and seven hours ahead of US Eastern Standard Time (EST). The clock moves forward one hour during daylight saving time, from the last Sunday in March until the last Sunday in October.

Electrical Appliances

Greece uses plugs with two round pins and an electrical voltage and frequency of 230 V/50Hz. UK devices will need adaptors; North American devices will need adaptors and voltage converters.

Driving Licences

All valid full European driving licences are accepted in Greece. If you are from outside the EU, you should get an International Driving Permit (IDP). To hire a car, you must be 21 or over, and you need to have a credit card and either a passport or ID card.

Weather

A Mediterranean climate means cool winters and hot, sunny summers. In peak season (Jul–Aug), temperatures can soar to 40º C (104º F). The coldest months are Jan–Feb, when temperatures occasionally drop to 0º C (32º F) and snow is rare but not unknown.

Language

Greek (Ellenika) is the official language, written using the Greek alphabet. Street signs are generally posted in both Greek and Latin characters. Most young people, especially those working in tourism, speak good English.

Smoking

In theory, smoking is prohibited in enclosed public spaces, including restaurants, nightclubs and offices, as well as in ferries and taxis. However, Greeks are heavy smokers (more than 40 per cent of the population smoke), and smoking remains quite common – in fact, many bar and café owners are reluctant to enforce non-smoking laws for fear of losing customers. In any case, if you visit Athens in summer you will probably eat and drink outdoors, so this should not be a problem if enclosed smoky spaces bother you.

Visitor Information

The **Greek National Tourism Organization (GNTO)** has a visitor information office at Dionysiou Areopagitou 18–20, opposite the Acropolis Museum (9am–8pm Mon–Fri, 10am–4pm Sat). Athens Airport has a smaller GNTO tourist office (9am–5pm Mon–Fri, 10am–4pm Sat). Both facilities give out maps and leaflets. The **This is Athens** website, run by the GNTO, is also useful.

DIRECTORY

POSTAL SERVICES
ELTA (Hellenic Post)
w elta.gr

NEWSPAPERS AND MAGAZINES
Athinorama (Greek only)
w athinorama.gr

Greece Is
w greece-is.com

Kathimerini (English version)
w ekathimerini.com

LiFO (Greek only)
w lifo.gr

VISITOR INFORMATION
Athens Development and Destination Management Agency
w developathens.gr

City of Athens Convention & Visitors Bureau
w athensconvention bureau.gr

Greek National Tourism Organization
w visitgreece.gr

Municipality of Athens
w cityofathens.gr

This is Athens
w thisisathens.org

Disabled Travellers

Although there have been massive improvements here, Greece still has a long way to go in terms of catering for the needs of disabled travellers. Some of the main attractions, such as the Acropolis and the Acropolis Museum, offer wheelchair access, but in general facilities are limited. Only a few hotels offer rooms specially designed for those with impaired mobility. However, Athens metro stations are equipped with lifts large enough for those using wheelchairs, and disabled visitors enjoy free entry to state-run archaeological sites and museums.

Organisations such as **Accessible Travel Greece** and **Sage Traveling** offer good help and advice for disabled travellers.

Trips and Tours

There are countless ways to explore Athens' impressive historical sites. If you wish to hire a private guide, you should contact the **Association of Licensed Tourist Guides**, which has a directory of qualified guides, with detailed profiles online, so you can choose someone who specializes in the fields you want to explore.

Alternatively, you can join the **Athens Open Tour**, which operates yellow open-top double-decker buses running a circular 90-minute tour, starting from Syntagma Square and taking in the city's main attractions, including the Acropolis, Acropolis Museum, the Benaki Museum and the National Archaeological Museum. Buses run daily, every 30 minutes (8am– 7:30pm Apr–Nov and 9am–5:30pm Dec– Mar). You can get on or off at any of the 14 stops, and the ticket is valid for 24 hours.

Active visitors might prefer **Athens by Bike**, which offers a guided bicycle tour around the main historic sites in the capital, starting at the Acropolis Museum and covering 9 km (5 miles) in three hours, departing daily at 10am and 2pm.

For something more quirky, both **Alternative Athens** and **Alternative Tours of Athens** offer amusing and informative tours giving an insight into the local lifestyle, with themes such as street art and food shopping. Likewise, the Canada-based company **Tours by Locals** can organize local freelance guides offering specialist private tours through an online booking service. **Discover Greek Culture** and **Athens Insiders** are great options for history, food and culture lovers.

Shopping

Shopping in Athens is fun and colourful, especially if you're looking for gifts to bring home. Typical Greek souvenirs include regional wines, olive oil, honey, *flokati* (shaggy woollen rugs), traditional copper coffee pots and hand-made wooden back-gammon sets. The best areas to look for these are Plaka and Monastiraki. Replicas of Ancient Greek finds – such as ceramic vases, or gold and silver jewellery – are for sale in some museum shops. The most atmospheric shopping venue has to be the Central Market, a series of covered halls on Athinas, between Monastiraki Square and Omonia Square. Shop here for local seasonal fruit and vegetables. A feast for the eyes, the market is a great spot for photos, too.

For designer clothing, accessories and jewellery, head for the upmarket boutiques in Kolonaki. If these are beyond your budget, join the locals on pedestrian-only Ermou, where you'll find all the big European chain-stores, such as Zara, Benetton and Promod.

Dining

Greeks love to eat out, so despite the economic crisis, Athens' restaurants and cafés are still thriving. In fact, dining out is integral to socializing – Greeks generally order a selection of dishes and share them, eating, drinking and chatting for several hours, with plates appearing and disappearing during the course of the meal, with less definition between the courses than there would be in most other European countries.

Various types of eatery serve specific foods. Go to a *psistaria* for spit-roasted and chargrilled meats, such as souvlaki, which are served as take-away snacks, or to a *mezedopoleio* for small platters of mezedes (tasty savoury snacks) served with ouzo or carafes of barrel wine.

ion »ion »ion » 143

A taverna is an informal rustic eatery serving hearty traditional cooking, while a *psarotaverna* is a taverna that specializes in fish and seafood dishes. At the top end of the scale, price-wise, an *estiatorio* is a fine-dining restaurant, offering formal service and a more structured menu with several courses, along with quality wines by the bottle.

Greeks tend to eat their meals later than most countries. Restaurants serve lunch noon–4pm and dinner 8pm–midnight. Some eateries serve meals all day long and do not close between lunch and dinner.

Where to Stay

Athens has a wide range of places to sleep. Prestigious five-star hotels offering old-fashioned elegance and extras such as rooftop swimming pools are to be found around Syntagma, close to the Parliament building. For sightseeing, touristy Plaka and the adjoining areas of Makrigianni and Koukaki, are ideal bases, thanks to their proximity to the Acropolis. Here you will find all types of accommodation, from mid-range boutique hotels in renovated Neo-Classical buildings with chic interiors, to basic but comfortable pensions and B&Bs. Likewise, Monastiraki and Psiri have hip boutique hotels offering personalized service, and crowded hostels with dormitories, in keeping with these neighbourhoods' gritty

downtown scene. Avoid Omonia, which is not totally safe at night – hence the cheaper room prices and mediocre hotels used by guided tour groups. Syngrou, although well located on the map, is a big, fast and noisy thoroughfare, and while the hotels here are functional and popular with business travellers, they offer little in the way of atmosphere or romance.

Over recent years, Athens has seen the opening of a dozen or so hostels aimed at young back-packers, as well as an increasing number of locals offering apartments to rent (complete with self-catering facilities), as well as individual rooms.

Hotels are designated star ratings by the **Hellenic Chamber of Hotels**. Prices vary depending on supply and demand, with high season generally viewed as Jul–Aug, when many foreign visitors stop in Athens for a couple of nights, before heading to the Greek islands. Rates generally include a continental buffet breakfast. The Hellenic Chamber of Hotels has instigated the revival of the long-forgotten traditional Greek breakfast, comprising yogurts, fruit, home-baked pies and regional specialities such as cheeses and sausages.

There are countless websites for choosing and booking your accommodation in Athens. These include **Hotels.com** and **Booking.com** for hotels, and **HostelWorld** for

hostels and budget accommodation. Sometimes, though, it's worth booking direct through the hotel or hostel website **Airbnb** is a great resource for apartments and private rooms. .

DIRECTORY

DISABLED TRAVELLERS
Accessible Travel Greece
W accessibletravel.gr

Sage Traveling
W sagetraveling.com

TRIPS AND TOURS
Alternative Athens
W alternativeathens.com

Alternative Tours of Athens
W atathens.org

Association of Licensed Tourist Guides
W tourist-guides.gr

Athens by Bike
W athensbybike.gr

Athens Insiders
W athensinsiders.com

Athens Open Tour
W athensopentour.com

Discover Greek Culture
W discovergreekculture.com

Tours by Locals
W toursbylocals.com

DINING
Culinary Backstreets
W culinarybackstreets.com

Greek Breakfast
W greekbreakfast.gr

WHERE TO STAY
Airbnb
W airbnb.com

Booking.com
W booking.com

Hellenic Chamber of Hotels
W grhotels.gr

Hotels.com
W hotels.com

HostelWorld
W hostelworld.com

Places to Stay

PRICE CATEGORIES
For a standard, double room per night (with breakfast if included), taxes and extra charges.

€ under €80   €€ €80–200   €€€ over €200

Luxury and High-End Hotels

Divani Caravel
MAP G5 ▪ Vasileos Alexandrou 2, Pangrati ▪ 210 720 7000 ▪ www.divanis.com ▪ €€
The lobby is decorated with antiques and marble, and the rooms are fitted out with every business amenity. Some 35 rooms have Acropolis views. There are bars and restaurants, and a rooftop garden with an indoor/outdoor pool. A free shuttle takes you to Syntagma.

The Hilton
MAP F4 ▪ Vasilissis Sofias 46, Ilissia ▪ 210 728 1000 ▪ www.hilton.com ▪ €€
The well-situated Athens Hilton is smart, functional and modern. Facilities include six restaurants, two bars (one on the rooftop), a swimming pool and a health centre, plus some extensive conference amenities.

NJV Athens Plaza
MAP M3 ▪ Vas. Georgiou A2 & Stadiou ▪ 210 335 2400 ▪ www.njvathens plaza.gr ▪ €€
Smack in the centre of town, this hotel has beautiful designer rooms with marble bathrooms, massage showers and Bulgari toiletries, plus a famously elegant lobby. Rooms on the eighth and ninth floors have great views of the Acropolis.

Radisson Blu Park Hotel
MAP D1 ▪ Leoforos Alexandras 10, Exarchia ▪ 210 889 4500 ▪ www.rbathenspark.com ▪ €€
Overlooking the lush greenery of Pediou tou Areos, this smart hotel has 152 rooms and suites decorated in subtle hues, each with a grey marble bathroom. Rooftop pool and fitness centre.

St George Lycabettus
MAP F3 ▪ Kleomenous 2, Kolonaki ▪ 210 741 6000 ▪ www.sglycabettus.gr ▪ €€
At this chic 154-room hotel built into the pine-scented slopes of Lykavittos Hill, full use is made of the rooftop, with an excellent restaurant, a swimming pool and a bar all sharing the views. A minibus service will whisk you to Plateia Syntagma.

Athenaeum Inter-Continental
MAP T2 ▪ Syngrou 89–93, Neos Kosmos ▪ 210 920 6000 ▪ www.inter continental.com ▪ €€€
Well-equipped, modern and stylish, if a little lacking in character. The excellent business facilities make this hotel a popular choice with executives, who probably also appreciate the gym, sauna, pool and shuttle to the city centre.

Divani Apollon Palace & Thalasso
MAP T3 ▪ Ag. Nikolaou 10 & Iliou, Vouliagmeni ▪ 210 891 1100 ▪ www.divanis.com ▪ €€€
A vast seaside hotel, with spacious rooms adorned with oak furniture and marble bathrooms. The complex has a private beach, and there are also outdoor and indoor pools. A shuttle bus serves Plateia Syntagma.

Electra Palace
MAP L4 ▪ Navarchou Nikodimou 18–20, Plaka ▪ 210 337 0000 ▪ www.electrahotels.gr ▪ €€€
This stylish hotel, probably the nicest in Plaka, has a mock Neo-Classical façade. The rooftop pool, with Acropolis views, is a great place to cool off after a day of sightseeing.

Hotel Grande Bretagne
MAP M3 ▪ Vas. Georgiou A1, Syntagma ▪ 210 333 0000 ▪ www.grande bretagne.gr ▪ €€€
With its marble lobby and glittering chandeliers, this establishment exudes timeless luxury. The opulence continues through 320 rooms and suites, a rooftop restaurant and pool, and the fitness centre.

King George Palace
MAP M3 ▪ Vas. Georgiou A3, Syntagma ▪ 210 322 2210 ▪ www.kinggeorge palace.gr ▪ €€€
A former retreat of the rich and famous, this hotel offers 102 rooms and suites, all with marble bathrooms, and

all individually furnished with select antiques.

Boutique and Design Hotels

Coco Mat Athens
MAP P2 ▪ 36 Patriarchou Ioakeim, Kolonaki ▪ 210 723 0000 ▪ www.cocomat athens.com ▪ €€
The Greek mattress company Coco Mat runs several hotels showcasing its wonderful beds. This hotel has 39 rooms, all with wooden floors and fabrics in muted earthy tones, and bathrooms of grey marble or white tiles.

Emporikon Athens
MAP K3 ▪ Aiolou 27A, Monastiraki ▪ 210 325 5118 ▪ www.emporikon athenshotel.com ▪ €€
This Neo-Classical Emporikon Athens Hotel is set in a refurbished 19th-century landmark building located in the heart of a booming historic district, St Irene Square.

InnAthens
MAP L4 ▪ Georgiou Souri 3 & Filellinon, Syntagma ▪ 210 325 8555 ▪ www. innathens.com ▪ €€
Occupying a renovated Neo-Classical mansion, InnAthens has 22 rooms and suites with slick contemporary design and marble bathrooms. It centres on a peaceful courtyard a five-minute walk from Syntagma. The superb breakfast is made with local Greek produce.

O&B
MAP B3 ▪ Leokoriou 7, Psiri ▪ 210 331 2940 ▪ www.oandbhotel.com ▪ €€
Priding itself on personalized service,

this welcoming hotel has just 22 rooms and suites, with minimalist design in tones of cream and beige. The small bar-restaurant does a fantastic breakfast, and serves drinks and light meals all day. It's located in a grungy side street in Psiri, but it's only a 20-minute walk from the Acropolis.

Pallas Athena
MAP C3 ▪ Athinas 65, Athens ▪ 210 325 0900 ▪ www.grecotelpallas athena.com ▪ €€
Luxury boutique hotel situated in the centre of the city that prides itself on its great art displays. The walls of its family rooms are decorated with fun murals and the loft suites are filled with contemporary art and sculpture. It has an excellent restaurant, as well as a tasty breakfast.

Periscope Hotel
MAP P2 ▪ Charitos 22, Kolonaki ▪ 210 729 7200 ▪ www.periscope.athens hotels.it ▪ €€
With its minimalist shape and contemporary style, this hotel in the heart of the city has raised the bar for modern accommodation in Athens. Great facilities.

Semiramis Hotel
MAP T2 ▪ Charilaou Trikoupi 48, Kefalari, Kifissia ▪ 210 628 4400 ▪ www.semiramis athens.com ▪ €€
Orange, pink and lime-green predominate in this funky 51-room hotel designed by Karim Rashid. There's a heated outdoor pool and a fitness centre. A changing selection

of contemporary art is displayed in the lobby.

AthensWas
MAP K5 ▪ Dionysiou Areopagitou 5, Makrigianni ▪ 210 924 9954 ▪ www. athenswas.gr ▪ €€€
This 21-room hotel stands on a car-free promenade, a five-minute walk from the Acropolis Museum. It's furnished with pieces by important 20th-century designers such as Le Corbusier and Eileen Gray, giving it a retro-chic vibe. The bathrooms are slick and spacious; breakfast is cooked to order and delicious.

The Margi Hotel
MAP T3 ▪ Litous 11, Vouliagmeni ▪ 210 892 9000 ▪ www.themargi.gr ▪ €€€
A five-minute walk from Vouliagmeni beach, this gem of a hotel comprises 89 rooms and suites, decorated in warm hues, with 19th-century antiques and marble bathrooms. The lounge bar is where guests relax in the evenings on poolside sofas.

New Hotel
MAP L4 ▪ Filellinon 16, Syntagma ▪ 210 327 3000 ▪ www.yeshotels.gr ▪ €€€
In the former Olympic Palace Hotel, the New Hotel stands a 10-minute walk from Syntagma. The 79 rooms have bamboo floors and quirky recycled furniture created by the Brazilian Campana brothers. Cooked-to-order breakfast and Sunday brunch are served in the New Taste restaurant.

Mid-Range Hotels

A for Athens
MAP J3 ▪ Miaouli 2–4, Monastiraki ▪ 210 324 4244 ▪ www.aforathens. com ▪ €€
This boutique hotel with 35 rooms is just across from the Acropolis, so guests enjoy unique views of this ancient monument even while they take a shower. Contemporary design and a relaxed, minimalist ambience.

Acropolis Select
MAP C6 ▪ Falirou 37–9, Koukaki ▪ 210 921 1610 ▪ www.acropoliselect.gr ▪ €€
One of the best deals in town: for only a little more than a budget hotel, you get a stylish lobby and restaurant, comfortable rooms, satellite TV, business amenities and, Acropolis views. Though not in a tourist neighbourhood, it's within an easy walk of most sights.

Adrian
MAP J3 ▪ Adrianou 74, Plaka ▪ 210 322 1553 ▪ www.douros-hotels. com ▪ €€
The Adrian offers rooms that are small and clean, if somewhat sterile, next to Hadrian's Library. The rooms have balconies, and the roof garden has lovely views. The café-filled square below is a nice place to sit, but it can get noisy at night.

Athens Center Square
MAP J2 ▪ Aristogeitonos 15, Monastiraki ▪ 210 322 2706 ▪ www.athens centersquarehotel.gr ▪ €€
Friendly and welcoming, this hotel has a downtown location, opposite the Central Market, giving it an authentic urban vibe. There are 54 colour-themed rooms with wooden floors and decent bathrooms, and a rooftop terrace with good views of the Acropolis and Lykavittos Hill. The price includes a generous buffet breakfast.

Athens Cypria
MAP L3 ▪ Diomeias 5, Syntagma ▪ 210 323 8034–8 ▪ www.athens cypria.com ▪ €€
Located just steps away from the bustle of Syntagma and the top-notch shopping of Ermou, the Cypria's rooms are simple, clean and comfortable, if a little bland and uniform. A hearty breakfast buffet is served until 10am.

Central Hotel
MAP L3 ▪ Apollonos 21, Plaka ▪ 210 323 4357 ▪ www.centralhotel.gr ▪ €€
Modern, minimalist and smart, the Central is one of the most reasonably priced hotels for its quality and location. Relax in the rooftop Jacuzzi with a view of the Acropolis and the mountains beyond.

Hermes
MAP L3 ▪ Apollonos 19, Syntagma ▪ 210 323 5514 ▪ www.hermes hotel.gr ▪ €€
The Hermes has 45 rooms with wooden floors and cheerful contemporary design. Some rooms are interconnected, making them ideal for families, and there's a playroom for small kids, plus babysitting on request.

A plentiful buffet breakfast, based on typical Greek produce, is also included.

Herodion
MAP C6 ▪ Rovertou Galli 4, Makrigianni ▪ 210 923 6832 ▪ www.herodion.gr ▪ €€
In a quiet neighbourhood just below the Acropolis, this attractive, modern hotel has comfortable rooms, the pale green and light wood accents of which feel cool and relaxing after a day touring the sights. Other features include Internet connection in every room and a flower-filled breakfast atrium.

Hotel Plaka
MAP K3 ▪ Kapnikareas 7 & Mitropoleos, Monastiraki ▪ 210 322 2706 ▪ www.plakahotel. gr ▪ €€
This hotel represents excellent value – for its unbeatable location between Plaka and the shopping street of Ermou, but also for its warm and simple but stylish rooms. The roof garden looks out to the Acropolis.

Philippos Hotel
MAP K6 ▪ Mitseon 3, Makrigianni ▪ 210 922 3611 ▪ www.philippos hotel.gr ▪ €€
In a peaceful residential side street, close to the Acropolis Museum, this family-run hotel is welcoming, peaceful and comfortable. The 50 rooms and suites are light and airy – most have balconies, some have Acropolis views. There is an adequate continental breakfast, but no restaurant as such.

Budget Hotels and Hostels

Art Gallery Hotel
MAP C6 ■ Erechthiou 5, Koukaki ■ 210 923 8376 ■ www.artgalleryhotel.gr ■ €

The priciest of the budget options, this hotel a short walk from the Acropolis and several good restaurants offers nice wooden floors and art in every room. There are low monthly rates in the off season. Breakfast costs extra.

Athens Choice
MAP C2 ■ Veranzerou 45, Omonia ■ 210 523 8738 ■ www.athenschoice.com ■ €

This hostel has a modern minimalist look in greys and charcoal. It has private rooms and shared dorms (sleeping four), a bar, TV lounge and laundry service, plus breakfast included. It's a five-minute walk from Omonia metro station (a little sleazy at night), near the National Archaeological Museum.

City Circus Hostel
MAP J2 ■ Sarri 16, Psiri ■ 213 023 7244 ■ www.citycircus.gr ■ €

In a renovated Neo-Classical mansion complete with frescoed ceilings, wrought-iron balconies and vintage furniture, retro-chic City Circus is a five-minute walk from Monastiraki metro station. Welcoming and tidy, it has private doubles and shared dorms sleeping four, six or eight, a restaurant and an Acropolis-view roof terrace.

Hotel Exarchion
MAP D2 ■ Themisto-kleous 55, Exarcheia ■ 210 380 0731 ■ www.exarchion.com ■ €

A fixture on the international backpacking circuit. Rooms are sparse but well kept, prices are low, the staff are friendly and the small outdoor bar is in the centre of lively, student-filled Plateia Exarcheia.

Marble House Pension
MAP B6 ■ An. Zinni 35, Koukaki ■ 210 923 4058 ■ www.marblehouse.gr ■ €

A favourite of students and artists, Marble House has clean, simple rooms and a friendly atmosphere. It offers discounted tours and monthly rates in the off season. Guests pay extra for air conditioning and a private bathroom.

Tempi Hotel
MAP J2 ■ Aiolou 29, Monastiraki ■ 210 321 3175 ■ www.tempihotel.gr ■ €

This family-run budget hotel is located in one Athens' up and coming neighbourhoods, St Irene Square in Monastiraki. Situated within walking distance to the major sights of Athens; expect clean, simple and comfortable rooms as well as a rooftop terrace along with a guest kitchen.

Athens Backpackers
MAP L5 ■ Makri 12, Makrigianni ■ 210 922 4044 ■ www.backpackers.gr ■ €€

This hostel offers two-, six- and eight-bed dorms, and the ensuing social life makes it hugely popular. Nearby offshoot Athens Studios has apartments for three to six people.

Athens Studios
MAP K6 ■ Veikou 3A, Makrigianni ■ 210 923 5811 ■ www.athens studios.gr ■ €€

Managed by the same people who run Athens Backpackers, this is close to the Acropolis Museum. The private studios and apartments (sleeping two, four or six) are ideal for couples or families and come with fully equipped kitchens and small ensuite bathrooms. Shared dorms for up to six people are also available. Continental breakfast is included.

AthenStyle
MAP J3 ■ Agias Theklas 10, Monastiraki ■ 210 322 5010 ■ www.athenstyle.com ■ €€

Choose from four- or six-bed dorms, private rooms or junior suites at this hotel within walking distance of the main sights. There are also breathtaking views of the Acropolis from the rooftop bar, which runs a very popular happy hour.

Hotel Phaedra
MAP L5 ■ Cherefontos 16, Plaka ■ 210 323 8461 ■ www.hotelphaedra.com ■ €€

This small, family-run hotel features balconies overlooking a church or the Acropolis. The rooms are tastefully furnished, and some have private bathrooms across the hall. The Phaedra's great rooftop terrace offers magnificent views. Known for its friendly staff.

For a key to hotel price categories see p144

High-End Hotels Outside Athens

Kastalia Boutique Hotel
MAP Q1 ▪ Vasileos Pavlou & Friderikis 13, Delphi ▪ 2265 082 205 ▪ www.kastaliahotel.gr ▪ €

Set in a renovated Neo-Classical mansion, this cosy boutique hotel stands just a five-minute walk from Delphi's archaeological site. It has 28 rooms and suites, a lounge with an open fireplace, and a stone terrace where breakfast is served, looking down on to the gorge and the sea.

Bratsera
MAP S4 ▪ Harbour, Hydra ▪ 2298 053 971 ▪ Mar–Oct ▪ www.bratserahotel.com ▪ €€

This hotel housed in a former sponge factory is one of the most charming places to stay in all of Greece. The quaint rooms and flower-filled courtyard are lovely, and there's also an outdoor pool.

Elatos Resort & Health Club
MAP R1 ▪ Itamos, nr Arachova ▪ 2234 061 162 ▪ www.elatos.com ▪ €€

Greece's only alpine resort is set in a pine forest at the edge of Parnassos National Park. All 40 chalets have two to three bedrooms, kitchens, fireplaces and verandas. The central buildings offer a fully equipped health club, bar and restaurant.

Poseidon Resort
MAP R2 ▪ Loutraki Korinthias, Loutraki ▪ 2744 067 938 ▪ www.poseidonresort.gr ▪ €€

This resort has a small private beach and extensive gardens, as well as sporting, spa and conference facilities. Accommodation varies widely in size, style and luxury, from individual rooms to villas. The bungalows are best, with their shiny wooden floors and cotton canopies.

Thermae Sylla Grand Hotel
MAP S1 ▪ Edipsos, North Evia ▪ 2226 060 100 ▪ www.thermaesyllaspa-hotel.com ▪ €€

One of the best spas in Greece, the Thermae Sylla offers treatments featuring Evia's restor-ative mineral-laden spring waters, along with a wide array of beauty and relaxation treat-ments. The beautiful external architecture has been preserved, but rooms and treatment areas are fully modern.

Amphitryon Hotel
MAP R3 ▪ Spiliadou, Nafplio ▪ 2752 070 700 ▪ www.amphitryon.gr ▪ €€€

Situated in Nafplio's Old Town, this smart hotel overlooks the sea, with a view of the Bourtzi (fortified islet). The 45 rooms have slick contemporary design, with wooden floors and marble-tiled bathrooms, while the Circle restaurant serves Mediterranean cuisine. Amphitryon is a member of Leading Small Hotels of the World.

Grand Resort Lagonissi
MAP T3 ▪ 40th km on the Athens–Sounio road, Lagonissi ▪ 2291 076 000 ▪ www.lagonissiresort.gr ▪ €€€

This vast resort complex spreads out over its own peninsula between Sounio and Vouliagmeni. It encompasses 16 beaches, with a range of seafront suites and lavish villas with their own pools. There are also a host of restaurants and organized activities.

Grecotel Cape Sounio
MAP T3 ▪ 67th km on the Athens–Sounio Rd ▪ 2292 069 700 ▪ www.grecotel.gr ▪ €€€

Offering all the mod cons you'd expect following a total overhaul, this branch of the Grecotel chain is set on a verdant hillside, with spectacular views of the sea and the Temple of Poseidon.

Nikki Beach Resort & Spa
MAP S4 ▪ Porto Heli, Argolis ▪ 2754 098 500 ▪ www.nikkibeachhotels.com ▪ €€

This 1970s beachfront hotel reopened in 2015 following a renovation. It has 66 spacious suites, all with minimalist white decor, lots of mirrors and stunning sea views. Some have private infinity pools. There is a beach, two pools (one featuring a swim-up cocktail bar), two rest-aurants, a spa and a gym.

Orloff Resort
Off map ▪ Spetses ▪ 2298 075 444 ▪ www.orloffresort.com ▪ €€€

This stylish boutique hotel is housed in a

19th-century mansion with an outdoor pool. The 19 rooms, studios and apartments combine traditional Greek architecture with modern minimalist design.

Mid and Budget Outside Athens

Aeginitiko Archontiko
MAP S3 ▪ Thomaidou & Agiou Nikolaou, Agia Marina, Aegina ▪ 2297 024 968 ▪ €
A 19th-century mansion with loads of character: painted ceilings, a parlour featuring stained-glass windows, and a garden courtyard. Rooms are small and clean, albeit with some peeling paint and banging pipes.

Arahova Inn
MAP R1 ▪ Central Arachova ▪ 2267 031 353 ▪ www.arahova-inn.gr ▪ €
Although the location is central, this hotel manages to feel relaxing and tranquil. It is a good base for accessing the ski resorts of Delphi and Parnassos.

Archontiko Art Hotel
MAP Q1 ▪ Visithra, near the harbour, Galaxidi ▪ 2265 042 292 ▪ www. archontikoarthotel.gr ▪ €
The themed rooms here sound a little kitschy but most manage to work. The "Bridal" has a huge canopy bed draped with sheer white linen; the "At Sea" is decorated like a boat; while adventurous couples go for the "Conception", featuring a round bed and mirrored ceiling. When not enjoying their rooms, guests can stroll in the pleasant garden.

Hotel Belle Helene
MAP R3 ▪ Christou Tsounta 15, Mycenae ▪ 2751 076 225 ▪ €
German archaeologist Heinrich Schliemann stayed here (in room No. 3) while excavating Mycenae in the 1870s, and many a classicist has followed in his footsteps. Modern-day tourists can enjoy clean, quiet, comfortable rooms in addition to the hotel's interesting historical significance.

Hotel Ganimede
MAP Q1 ▪ Gourgouri 20, Galaxidi ▪ 2265 041 328 ▪ www.ganimede.gr ▪ €
The rooms in this 19th-century mansion are simple but elegant; however, the real draw is the combination of a lovely courtyard garden overflowing with fragrant flowers, the sumptuous breakfasts and the warm hospitality of the Italian owners.

Hotel Tholos
MAP Q1 ▪ Apollonos 31, Delphi ▪ 2265 082 268 ▪ www.tholoshotel.com ▪ €
This is a good budget option in Delphi. Rooms are cheap, clean and nicely furnished, and the owners are friendly.

King Othon
MAP R3 ▪ Farmakopoulou 4, Nafplion ▪ 2752 027 585 ▪ www.kingothon.gr ▪ €
Located in a two-storey Neo-Classical building with delightfully painted ceilings, this hotel is near the centre of old Nafplio. Rooms come in several sizes, and breakfast includes home-baked goodies.

Parnassos Hotel
MAP Q1 ▪ V. Pavlos 32, Delphi ▪ 2265 082 321 ▪ www.parnassos.org ▪ €
This family-run hotel offers a good range of facilities, such as air conditioning, central heating, satellite TV and Wi-Fi. It is close to Delphi and convenient for skiing at Mount Parnassos, swimming at Galaxidi and Itea, or visiting the area's museums.

Pension Marianna
MAP R3 ▪ Ilia Potamianou 9, Nafplio ▪ 2752 024 256 ▪ www.hotelmarianna.gr ▪ €
Located in Nafplio's car-free Old Town, this welcoming hotel is quaint and romantic. Centering around a lovely courtyard, it has 20 rooms, all decorated in warm shades of yellow, orange and red. A home-made breakfast is served on a rooftop patio, directly below the fortress, with some lovely views over the town and out to sea.

Klymeni Traditional Homes
MAP R3 ▪ 25th Martiou & Karamanli, Nafplio ▪ 2752 096 194 ▪ www.klymeni.gr ▪ €€
Offering accommodation in a range of rustic-chic studios, bungalows and apartments built of local natural stone, Klymeni is set in gardens with a barbecue, a hot tub and a children's play area. Surrounded by rural farmland, it's totally peaceful, located just 1.5 km (1 mile) inland from Nafplio's Old Town.

For a key to hotel price categories see p144

General Index

Acknowledgments

Author
Coral Davenport and Jane Foster are freelance travel and features writers, based in Athens.

Additional contributor
Cordelia Madden

Publishing Director Georgina Dee

Publisher Vivien Antwi

Design Director Phil Ormerod

Editorial Michelle Crane, Rachel Fox, Freddie Marriage, Adrian Potts, Sally Schafer, Sands Publishing Solutions, Hollie Teague

Design Marisa Renzullo, Stuti Tiwari, Vinita Venugopal

Commissioned Photography Courtesy of ARF/TAP (Archaeological Receipts Fund), Nigel Hicks, Courtesy of Kori 69b, Rob Reichenfeld, Rough Guides/Chris Christoforo, Rough Guides/Michelle Grant.

Picture Research Ellen Root, Lucy Sienkowska, Rituraj Singh

Cartography Mohammad Hassan, Zafar-ul-Islam Khan, Suresh Kumar, James Macdonald, John Plumer

DTP Jason Little, Azeem Siddiqui

Production Luca Bazzoli

Factchecker Marisa Tejada

Proofreader Clare Peel

Indexer Hilary Bird

First edition created by Blue Island Publishing, London

Picture Credits

123RF.com: Anastasios Anestis 83cla; Sergii Figurnyi 132tr; Milan Gonda 77br; gzach 34br; Maxim Krivoshein 123tl; Stefanos Kyriazis 77t.
4Corners: Mel Manser 13crb; Gianluca Santoni 57tl, 87cl.
Alamy Stock Photo: age fotostock/Gonzalo Azumendi 96br, /Alvaro Leiva 17tc; Alpineguide 2tl, 8-9; A. Amsel 79tl; Art Directors & TRIP/Helene Rogers 129cr; The Art Archive/Gianni Dagli Orti 18ca, 47cl; charistoone-travel 31clb; Richard Cummins 110cla; Fine Arts/INTERFOTO 102bl; Peter Forsberg 88tl; funkyfood London - Paul Williams 1, 3tl, 4t, 74-5; Glyn Genin 103cl;
Greek Photonews 12cl; GreekStock 111tr; Peter Grumann 63b; Terry Harris 61cl, 72cl, 84br, 104cla; Chris Hellier 119tl; hemis.fr/ Paule Seux 4cr; Heritage Image Partnership Ltd/Fine Art Images 26cl, /Sites & Photos 25tl; Peter Horree 23crb; Constantinos Iliopoulos 70tl; Imageplotter 18crb; IML Image Group 31br, /Velissarios Voutsas 33br; INTERFOTO 51cla, 55tc; Art Kowalsky 4cla; Lanmas 40b; Hercules Milas 4b, 34-5, 54b, 112cr, 112-3, 118crb, 129t; nagelestock. com 7tr; Odyssey-Images 68clb; Steve Outram 72tr; Nikos Pavlakis 70b, 94b; Pictorial Press Ltd 43bl; Prisma Archivo 19cr; Prisma Bildagentur AG/Schultz Reinhard 41cla; Sklifas Steven 11cla, 30br, 30-1, 37tr; Ken Welsh 4crb; Jan Wlodarczyk 2tr, 38-9, 102t; World History Archive 46t; ZUMA Press, Inc. 45br.
Aleria Restaurant: 64br.
Alternative Athens: Eftychia Vlachou 62bl.
AWL Images: Hemis 3tr, 108-9, 134-5; Jane Sweeney 28-9, 60b.
Benaki Museum Athens: 11tr, 26crb, 27cla, 27crb.
Booze Cooperative: 91br.
Bridgeman Images: Epigraphical Museum, Archaelogical Museum, Athens, De Agostini Picture Library/Archivio J. Lange 93c.
Museum of the City of Athens: 93br.
Corbis: Richard Cummins 71tr, 111br; Demotix/Kostas Pikoulas 73cl; EPA/Yannis Kolesidis 50cr, /Orestis Panagiotou 77cl, 93tl; Macduff Everton 95cl; JAI/Walter Bibikow 17br; Keystone/Georgios Kefalas14tl, 15b; Leemage 10c; Francis G. Mayer 46bl; Daniella Nowitz 33tl; Thierry Orban 42t; Paul Panayiotou 82b; Ted Spiegel 44br.
Dreamstime.com: Absente 117br, 120b; Abxyz 40c; Anastasios71 6cl; Leonid Andronov 55br; Artistique7 17cr; Jennifer Barrow 10cla; Pavla Bartonova 30clb; Sergio Bertino 20crb; Daniel Boiteau 36br; Boris Breytman 122tl; Corluc 48cl; Dimaberkut 72br, 100tr, 104br; Igor Dutina 90cb; Edwardgerges 15tl, 96tl; Elgreko74 53tl, 63cla; Alexandre Fagundes De Fagundes 55cl, 76tl; Foodio 67cl; Gelia 118tl; Dimitrios Giannopoulos 130tl; Gmoulart 120t; Milan Gonda 84cla, 86b, 112bl; Antonio Gravante 43tr; Stoyan Haytov 119br; Theodoros Ikramidis 24br; Imagin.gr Photography 12tr, 124tl, 132bl; Gabriela Insuratelu 128tl, 131cl; Ivandzyuba 115t; Kmiragaya 44tc; Dimitris Kolyris 11crb, 52clb; Bo Li 12bc; Littlewormy 10ca; Lkpro555 4clb; Lornet 49b, 60tl; Galina Mikhalishina 61tr; Predrag Milosavljevic 66bl; Milosk50 78b; Minadezhda 66c; Niradj 66tr; Odua 83crb; Pantelis V. 116c; Lefteris Papaulakis 10crb, 11bl, 16-7, 20-1, 24-5, 47br, 56b, 117tl, 126bl;

Emmanouil Pavlis 19b, 35tl; Photostella 71cl, 85tl; Rhombur 36-7; Rosshelen 16bl; Sborisov 12-3, 101clb; Jozef Sedmak 57crb; Nikolai Sorokin 53b, 115cb, 124b; George Tsartsianidis 67tl; Valery109 24cla; Bruce Whittingham 68tr,130b; Yoemll 34tl; Angel Yordanov 123b.

Epikouros Restaurant - Taverna: 121cr.

Floral: 99t.

Folli Follie: www.imagepro.gr/S Efstathopoulos 105t

Getty Images: AFP PHOTO/Louisa Gouliamaki 21bc; Allan Baxter 4cl; 58-9; DEA /A. Garozzo 79clb, /G. Nimatallah 18cl, /G. Dagli Orti 21crb; Slow Images 86cla; George Tsafos 78cla, 88crb; Universal Images Group 11cr.

Nicholas P Goulandris Foundation - Museum of Cycladic Art: 10bl, 22cla, 22c, 22br, 22-3, 23ca, 50tl.

Hilton Athens: Galaxy Bar & Restaurant 106t, Milos Restaurant 107cr.

Hytra: Kaplanidis Yirgos 65cl.

iStockphoto.com: efesenko 125cla.

Loumidis Coffee Shop: 97tl.

Marinos Restaurant: Lena Lo 127cl.

Martinos Antiques: 89tr.

Melissinos Art - The Poet Sandalmaker: 89c.

Nakas Musical Instruments: 97cr.

Nontas Fish Restaurant: 133cr.

Restaurant Spondi: 65tl.

Rex by Shutterstock: De Agostini/G. D Orti 92tl; Sharok Hatami 41br.

Rififi: 65br, 98br.

Robert Harding Picture Library: Massimo Pizzotti 20bl; Silwen Randebrock 26tr.

Photo Scala, Florence: 32cr; DeAgostini Picture Library/Veneranda Biblioteca Ambrosiana 49tl.

Six D.O.G.S: 91tl.

Skoumoky: 81t.

SuperStock: LatitudeStock/Capture Ltd 73tr.

Vassilenas Etolikou: 114br.

Warehouse: Themis Katsimihas 98cl.

WeArePress: 64cla.

Cover

Front and spine: Alamy Stock Photo: Bill Heinsohn.

Back: Dreamstime.com: Milosk50.

Pull Out Map Cover

Alamy Stock Photo: Bill Heinsohn
All other images © Dorling Kindersley
For further information see: www.dkimages.com

As a guide to abbreviations in visitor information blocks: **Adm** = admission charge; **DA** = disabled access; **D** = dinner; **L** = lunch.

Penguin Random House

Printed and bound in China

First American Edition, 2004

First published in the United States by Dorling Kindersley Limited 345 Hudson Street, New York, New York 10014

Copyright 2004, 2017 © Dorling Kindersley Limited

A Penguin Random House Company

18 19 20 10 9 8 7 6 5 4 3 2

Reprinted with revisions 2006, 2008, 2010, 2012, 2014, 2017

A CIP catalogue record is available from the British Library.

ISBN 978 1 4654 5990 9

ISSN 1479-344X

33614080785859

Paper from responsible sources
FSC™ C018179

SPECIAL EDITIONS OF DK TRAVEL GUIDES

Phrase Book

In an Emergency

Help!	Voítheia!	vo-ee-theea
Stop!	Stamatíste!	sta-ma-tee-steh
Call a doctor!	Fonáxte éna giatró!	fo-nak-steh e-na ya-tro
Call an ambulance/ the police/	Kaléste to asthenofóro/tin astynomía/tin	ka-le-steh to as-the-no-fo-ro teen a-sti-no-the mia/ teen pee-ro-zve-stee-kee!
fire brigade!	pyrosvestikí!	
Where is the nearest telephone/ hospital/ pharmacy?	Poú eínai to plisiéstero tiléfono/ nosokomeío/ farmakeío?	poo ee-ne to plee-see-e-ste-ro tee-le-pho-no/ no-so-ko-mee-o/ far-ma-kee-o

Communication Essentials

Yes	Nai	neh
No	Ochi	o-chee
Please	Parakaló	pa-ra-ka-lo
Thank you	Efcharistó	ef-cha-ree-sto
You are welcome	Parakaló	pa-ra-ka-lo
OK/alright	Entáxei	en-dak-zee
Excuse me	Me synchoreíte	me seen-cho-ree-teh
Hello	Geiá sas	yeea sas
Goodbye	Antío	an-dee-o
Good morning	Kaliméra	ka-lee-me-ra
Good night	Kalin'ychta	ka-lee-neech-ta
Morning	Proí	pro-ee
Afternoon	Apógevma	a-po-yev-ma
Evening	Vrádi	vrath-i
This morning	Símera to proí	see-me-ra to pro-ee
Yesterday	Chthés	chthes
Today	Símera	see-me-ra
Tomorrow	Avrio	av-ree-o
Here	Edó	ed-o
There	Ekeí	e-kee
What?	Tí?	tee
Why?	Giatí?	ya-tee
Where?	Poú?	poo
How?	Pós?	pos
Wait!	Perímene!	pe-ree-me-neh
How are you?	Tí káneis?	tee ka-nees
Very well, thank you.	Poly kalá, efcharistó.	po-lee ka-la, ef-cha-ree-sto
How do you do?		pos ees-te
Pleased to meet you.	Chaíro pol'y.	che-ro po-lee
What is your name?	Pós légeste?	pos le-ye-ste
	poo ee-ne	
Where is/are…?	Poú eínai…?	
How far is it to…?	Póso apéchei…?	po-so a-pe-chee
How do I get to…?	Pós mporó na páo…?	pos bo-ro na pa-o
Do you speak English?	Miláte Angliká?	mee-la-te an-glee-ka
I understand.	Katalavaíno.	ka-ta-la-ve-no
I don't understand.	Den katalavaíno.	den ka-ta-la-ve-no
Could you speak slowly?	Miláte lígo pio argá parakaló?	mee-la-te lee-go pyo ar-ga pa-ra-ka-lo
I'm sorry.	Me synchoreíte.	me seen-cho-ree-teh

Does anyone have a key?	Echei kanénas kleidí?	e-chee ka-ne-nas klee-dee

Useful Words

big	Megálo	me-ga-lo
small	Mikró	mi-kro
hot	Zestó	zes-to
cold	Kr'yo	kree-o
good	Kaló	ka-lo
bad	Kakó	ka-ko
enough	Arketá	ar-ke-ta
well	Kalá	ka-la
open	Anoichtá	a-neech-ta
closed	Kleistá	klee-sta
left	Aristerá	a-ree-ste-ra
right	Dexiá	dek-see-a
straight on	Eftheía	ef-thee-a
between	Anámesa / Metax'y	a-na-me-sa/ me-tak-see
on the corner of…	Sti gonía tou…	stee go-nee-a too
near	Kontá	kon-da
far	Makriá	ma-kree-a
up	Epáno	e-pa-no
down	Káto	ka-to
early	Norís	no-rees
late	Argá	ar-ga
entrance	I eísodos	ee ee-so-thos
exit	I éxodos	ee e-kso-dos
toilet	Oi toualétes / Kateiliméni	ee too-a-le-tes ka-tee-lee-me-nee
occupied/ engaged		
unoccupied	Eléftheri	e-lef-the-ree
free/no charge	Doreán	tho-re-an
in/out	Mésa/ Exo	me-sa/ek-so

Making a Telephone Call

Where is the nearest public telephone?	Poú vrísketai o plisiéstero tilefonikós thálamos?	poo vrees-ke-teh o plee-see-e-ste-ros tee-le-fo-ni-kos tha-la-mos
I would like to place a long-distance call.	Tha íthela na káno éna yperastikó tilefónima.	tha ee-the-la na ka-no e-na ee-pe-ra-sti-ko tee-le-fo-nee-ma.
I would like to reverse the charges.	Tha íthela na chreóso to tilefónima ston paralípti.	tha ee-the-la na chre-o-so to tee-le-fo-nee-ma ston pa-ra-lep-tee
I will try again later.	Tha xanatilefoníso argótera.	tha ksa-na-tee-le-fo-ni-so ar-go-te-ra
Can I leave a message?	Mporeíte na tou afísete éna mínyma?	bo-ree-te na too a-fee-se-teh e-na mee-nee-ma
Could you speak up a little please?	Miláte dynatótera, parakaló?	mee-la-teh dee-na-to-te-ra, pa-ra-ka-lo
Hold on.	Perímenete.	pe-ri-me-ne-teh
local call	Topikó tilefónima	to-pi-ko tee-le-fo-nee-ma
OTE telephone office	O OTE / To tilefoneío	o O-TE / To tee-le-fo-nee-o
phone box/ kiosk	O tilefonikós thálamos	o tee-le-fo-ni-kos tha-la-mos
phone card	I tilekárta	ee tee-le-kar-ta

Shopping

How much does this cost?	Póso kánei?	po-so ka-nee
I would like…	Tha íthela…	tha ee-the-la
Do you have…?	Echete…?	e-che-teh
I am just looking.	Aplós koitáo.	a-plos kee-ta-o
Do you take credit cards/ travellers' cheques?	Décheste pistotikés kártes/ travellers' cheques?	the-ches-teh pee-sto-tee-kes kar-tes/ travellers cheques
What time do you open/ close?	Póte anoígete/ kleínete?	po-teh a-nee-ye-teh/ klee-ne-teh
Can you ship this overseas?	Mporeíte na to steílete sto exoterikó?	bo-ree-teh na to stee-le-teh sto e-xo-te-ree-ko
This one.	Aftó edó.	af-to e-do
That one.	Ekeíno.	e-kee-no
expensive	Akrivó	a-kree-vo
cheap	Fthinó	fthee-no
size	To mégethos	to me-ge-thos
white	Lefkó	lef-ko
black	Mávro	mav-ro
red	Kókkino	ko-kee-no
yellow	Kítrino	kee-tree-no
green	Prásino	pra-see-no
blue	Mple	bleh

Sightseeing

tourist information	O EOT	o E-OT
tourist police	I touristikí astynomía	ee too-rees-tee-kee a-stee-no-mee-a
closed on public holidays	kleistó tis argíes	klee-sto tees aryee-es

Transport

When does the … leave?	Póte févgei to…?	po-teh fev-yee to
Where is the bus stop?	Poú eínai i stási tou leoforeíou?	poo ee-neh ee sta-see too le-o-fo-ree-oo
Is there a bus to…?	Ypárchei leoforeío gia…?	ee-par-chee le-o-fo-ree-o yia
ticket office	Ekdotíria eisitiríon	Ek-tho-tee-reea ee-see-tee-ree-on
return ticket	Eisitírio me epistrofí	ee-see-tee-ree-o meh e-pee-stro-fee
single journey	Apló eisitírio	a-plo ee-see-tee-reeo
bus station	O stathmós leoforeíon	o stath-mos leo-fo-ree-on
bus ticket	Eisitírio leoforeíou	ee-see-tee-ree-o leo-fo-ree-oo
trolley bus	To trólley	to tro-le-ee
port	To limán	to lee-ma-nee
train/metro	To tréno	to tre-no
railway station	sidirodromikós stathmós	see-thee-ro-thro-mee-kos stath-mos
moped	To moto- podílato/ To michanáki	to mo-to-po-thee-la-to/to mee-cha-na-kee
bicycle	To podílato	to po-thee-la-to
taxi	To taxí	to tak-see
airport	To aeródrómio	to a-e-ro-thro-mee-o

ferry	To "ferry-boat"	to fe-ree-bot
hydrofoil	To delfíni/ To ydroptérygo	to del-fee-nee/ To ee-throp-te-ree-go
catamaran for hire	To katamarán Enoikiázontai	to catamaran e-nee-kya-zon-deh

Staying in a Hotel

Do you have a vacant room?	Echete domátia?	e-che-teh tho-ma-tee-a
I have a reservation.	Echo kánei krátisi.	e-cho ka-nee kra-tee-see.
double room with double bed	Díklino me moná kreváti	thee-klee-no meh thee-plo kre-va-tee
twin room	Díklino me dipló kreváti	thee-klee-no meh mo-na kre-vat-ya
single room	Monóklino	mo-no-klee-no
room with a bath	Domátio me mpánio	tho-ma-tee-o meh ban-yo
shower	To douz	To dooz
porter	O portiéris	o por-tye-rees
key	To kleidí	to klee-dee
room with a sea view/balcony	Domátio me théa sti thálassa/ mpalkóni	tho-ma-tee-o meh the-a stee tha-la-sa/bal-ko-nee
Does the price include breakfast?	To proinó symperi- lamvánetai stin timí?	to pro-ee-no seem-be-ree-lam-va ne-teh steen tee-me

Eating Out

Have you got a table?	Echete trapézi?	e-che-te tra-pe-zee
I want to reserve a table.	Thélo na kratíso éna trapézi.	the-lo na kra-tee-so e-na tra-pe-zee
The bill, please.	Ton logariazmó parakaló.	ton lo-gar-yas-mo pa-ra-ka-lo
I am a vegetarian.	Eímai chortofágos.	ee-meh chor-to-fa-gos
What is fresh today?	Tí frésko échete símera?	tee fres-ko é-che-teh see-me-ra
waiter/waitress	K'yrie/Garson/ Kyría	Kee-ree-eh/ Gar-son/ Kee-ree-a
menu	O katálogos	o ka-ta-lo-gos
cover charge	To "couvert"	to koo-ver
wine list	O katálogos me ta oinopne- vmatódi	o ka-ta-lo-gos meh ta ee-no-pnev-ma-to-thee
glass	To potíri	to po-tee-ree
bottle	To mpoukáli	to bou-ka-lee
knife	To machaíri	to ma-che-ree
fork	To piroúni	to pee-roo-nee
spoon	To koutáli	to koo-ta-lee
breakfast	To proinó	to pro-ee-no
lunch	To mesi- merianó	to me-see-mer-ya-no
dinner	To deípno	to theep-no
main course	To kyríos gévma	to kee-ree-os yev-ma
starter/ first course	Ta orektiká	ta o-rek-tee-ka
dessert	To glykó	to ylee-ko

dish of the day	To piáto tis iméras	to pya-to tees ee-me-ras
bar	To "bar"	To bar
taverna	I tavérna	ee ta-ver-na
café	To kafeneío	to ka-fe-nee-o
fish taverna	I psarotavérna	ee psa-ro-ta-ver-na
grill house	I psistariá	ee psee-sta-rya
wine shop	To oinopoleío	to ee-no-po-lee-o
dairy shop	To galakto-poleío	to ga-lak-to-po-lee-o
restaurant	To estiatório	to e-stee-a-to-ree-o
ouzeri	To ouzerí	to oo-ze-ree
meze shop	To meze-dopoleío	To me-ze-do-po-lee-o
take away kebabs	To souvlatzí-diko	To soo-vlat-zee-dee-ko
rare	Eláchista psim-éno	e-lach-ees-ta psee-me-no
medium	Métria psiméno	met-ree-a psee-me-no
well done	Kalopsiméno	ka-lo-psee-me-no

Basic Food and Drink

coffee	O Kafés	o ka-fes
with milk	me gála	me ga-la
black coffee	skétos	ske-tos
without sugar	chorís záchari	cho-rees za-cha-ree
medium sweet	métrios	me-tree-os
very sweet	glykos	glee-kos
tea	tsái	tsa-ee
hot chocolate	zestí sokoláta	ze-stee so-ko-la-ta
wine	krasí	kra-see
red	kókkino	ko-kee-no
white	lefkó	lef-ko
rosé	rozé	ro-ze
water	To neró	to ne-ro
octopus	To chtapódi	to chta-po-dee
fish	To psári	to psa-ree
cheese	To tyrí	to tee-ree
halloumi	To chaloúmi	to cha-loo-mee
bread	To psomí	to pso-mee
houmous	To houmous	to choo-moos
halva	O chalvás	o chal-vas
meat kebabs	O g'yros	o yee-ros
Turkish delight	To loukoúmi	to loo-koo-mee
baklava ·	O mpaklavás	o bak-la-vas

Numbers

1	éna	e-na
2	d'yo	thee-o
3	tría	tree-a
4	téssera	te-se-ra
5	pénte	pen-deh
6	éxi	ek-si
7	eptá	ep-ta
8	ochtó	och-to
9	ennéa	e-ne-a
10	déka	the-ka
11	énteka	en-de-ka
12	dódeka	tho-the-ka
13	dekatría	de-ka-tree-a
14	dekatéssera	the-ka-tes-se-ra
15	dekapénte	the-ka-pen-de
16	dekaéxi	the-ka-ek-si
17	dekaeptá	the-ka-ep-ta
18	dekaochtó	the-ka-och-to
19	dekaennéa	the-ka-e-ne-a

20	eíkosi	ee-ko-see
21	eikosiéna	ee-ko-see-e-na
30	triánta	tree-an-da
40	saránta	sa-ran-da
50	penínta	pe-neen-da
60	exínta	ek-seen-da
70	evdomínta	ev-tho-meen-da
80	ogdónta	og-thon-da
90	enenínta	e-ne-neen-da
100	ekató	e-ka-to
200	diakósia	thya-kos-ya
1,000	chília	cheel-ya
2,000	d'yo chiliádes	thee-o cheel-ya-thes
1,000,000	éna ekatommýrio	e-na e-ka-to-mee-ree-o
one minute	éna leptó	e-na lep-to
one hour	mía óra	mee-a o-ra
half an hour	misí óra	mee-see o-ra
quarter of an hour	éna tétarto	e-na te-tar-to
half past one	mía kai misí	mee-a keh mee-see
quarter past one	mía kai tétarto	mee-a keh te-tar-to
ten past one	mía kai déka	mee-a keh the-ka
quarter to two	dýo pará tétarto	thee-o pa-ra te-tar-to
ten to two	dýo pará déka	thee-o pa-ra the-ka
a day	mía méra	mee-a me-ra
a week	mía evdomáda	mee-a ev-tho-ma-tha
a month	énas mínas	e-nas mee-nas
a year	énas chrónos	e-nas chro-nos
Monday	Deftéra	thef-te-ra
Tuesday	Tríti	tree-tee
Wednesday	Tetárti	te-tar-tee
Thursday	Pémpti	pemp-tee
Friday	Paraskeví	pa-ras-ke-vee
Saturday	Sávvato	sa-va-to
Sunday	Kyriakí	keer-ee-a-kee
January	Ianouários	ee-a-noo-a-ree-os
February	Fevrouários	fev-roo-a-ree-os
March	Mártios	mar-tee-os
April	Aprílios	a-pree-lee-os
May	Máios	ma-ee-os
June	Ioúnios	ee-oo-nee-os
July	Ioúlios	ee-oo-lee-os
August	Avgoustos	av-goo-stos
September	Septémvrios	sep-tem-vree-os
October	Októvrios	ok-to-vree-os
November	Noémvrios	no-em-vree-os
December	Dekémvrios	the-kem-vree-os